Sally Stanford

California's Grand Bordello House Madam

Alton Pryor

Stagecoach Publishing
5360 Campcreek Loop
Roseville, Ca. 95747
stagecoach@surewest.net

Sally Stanford

California's Grand Bordello House Madam

Copyright Alton Pryor 2019

ISBN: 978-1-7923-0382-1

Stagecoach Publishing
5360 Campcreek Loop
Roseville, Ca. 95747
stagecoach@surewest.net

"If I hadn't been President of the United States, I probably would have ended up a piano player in a bawdy house."

Harry S. Truman

Table of Contents

1

Her Bootlegging Days

Sally Stanford was the Queen of Sin in San Francisco's halcyon days of the 1930s. She was both a bootlegger and a brothel madam during the prohibition years.

The illustrious madam was named Mabel Janice Busby at birth in Baker City, Oregon, a small farm community. (In her writings she simply referred to her hometown as Baker, Oregon) She termed her early years "as fighting starvation and poverty in an Oregon ditch".

"I didn't set out to be a madam any more than Arthur Michael Ramsey set out to be the Archbishop of Canterbury,"

Sally, opening in her book, *"The Lady of the House"* (1966), said, "At a time when most young girls decide to become schoolteachers, actresses, or lady lawyers, one doesn't say, *that's for me. I'm going to be a madam."*

Sally Stanford

As California's and perhaps the nation's most preeminent madam, Sally said, "I have never been the least bit touchy or sensitive about it."

Sally claimed her family was so poor "we envied everyone we ever heard of.

She seemed smart, funny and world wise, and carved an unconventional niche for herself, going from a third-grade dropout to a powerful executive in her later years.

Writing in her book, Sally said, "It doesn't take much to produce a good merchant of cash and carry love: just courage, an infinite capacity for perpetual suspicion, stamina on a 24-hour-a-day basis, the deathless conviction that the customer is always wrong, a fair knowledge of first and second aid, do it yourself gynecology, judo—and a tremendous sense of humor."

No one sets out to be a madam, but madams answer the call of a well-recognized and basic human need, she maintains. Before becoming a madam, Sally ventured into the productive but illegal bootlegging business.

Sally swears she did not smoke a cigarette or have a drink of alcohol until she was 46 years old. That didn't stop her from venturing into the bootlegging business.

"A lot of jokes have been made about bathtub gin, but there was never a container more convenient for the production of high-class hooch," she said. "In an emergency the plug could be pulled, and all the evidence went far out to sea."

Five gallons of alcohol cost twenty-five dollars. This had to be cut, flavored with bourbon extract, colored with caramel, bottled and labeled.

"I used to age mine for 48 hours," she said.

Sally said she wasn't a good enough chemist to produce good gin. "It was almost as cheap as Clorox at the time and far tastier."

She learned that by serving her guests salty chicken, it encouraged them to buy more drinks.

In her early San Francisco years, Sally set a determined goal. She would be the best San Francisco madam, hostess to movie stars, business moguls, and politicians, there was.

Her goal is not without precedent. It seems clear that prostitution is not the oldest profession as recorded by many historians. But it ranks right up there behind "Hunting and Gathering'.

Prostitution has existed in nearly every civilization on earth. Whenever there have been goods and services available for barter, somebody most likely bartered for sex.

Among Sally's major hates are the pimps that invade the prostitution business. She admits to wanting to eradicate them, calling them the "crabgrass" of prostitution.

"Pimps are always moving in where the green stuff is thickest."

Sally Stanford married six or seven times (depending on the source). At least three of her spouses thought they were her first. "Good old moral Christians like us can have all kinds of husbands or wives, as long as we keep them one at a time."

She points out that immoral Mohammedans can have as many wives as they can properly care for, a caper that our morality doesn't buy.

Sally asks, "Why is the bliss of ignorance considered so moral? My blood pressure goes up when more attention is paid to drilling young people on dental rather than sexual hygiene.

"Syphilis and gonorrhea could go the way of smallpox and scarlet fever. They could be eradicated in a matter of months if we didn't stick our heads in the sand."

Sally's was not the first house of prostitution in San Francisco. There were several other madams operating in the city.

There was, for example, "Diamond Jessie" Hayman. She called her Ellis Street house "an oasis from cares and time.

Her establishment operated from the 1890s to the time of Prohibition in 1919.

At the time, she called herself Jessie Mellon. She was a boarder at the Ellis Street house of Nina Hayman. Jessie, who was noted for her trysts with a Russian Grand Duke on a world tour. She took over both Madam Hayman's name and her business.

Diamond Jessie soon operated a chain of parlor houses. She was forced to close them in 1917 because of a crusade against vice by religious groups.

Jessie died in a London hotel while on a world tour.

Another San Francisco madam of fame was Tessie Wall, a blonde and flamboyant madam in San Francisco's Tenderloin District.

Tessie loved champagne and is said to have once outlasted boxer John L. Sullivan in a drinking bout while she worked as a dancehall girl.

Her first brothel was on Larkin Street. She then moved to O'Farrell Street. Her O'Farrell address was popular with young college-boy clientele.

Tessie married gambler Frank Daroux. The marriage broke up and they were divorced. Tessie, however, continued to carry the torch for Daroux.

When he refused to return to her, she shot him. Daroux survived. When Tessie was arrested, she shouted, "I shot him because I love him, God damn him!" Tessie retired with a fortune in 1932.

In her book, "Lady of the House", Sally Stanford said, "Madaming is the sort of thing that just happens to you—like getting a battlefield commission or becoming dean of women at Stanford University.

2

Her Poverty Days

Sally Stanford hated poverty in all its forms. As a youngster, she found that hanging about the local golf course could sometimes be remunerative.

Golfers were always losing their golf balls, which in those days were expensive. Many players never bothered to hunt the balls they considered lost.

Sally used to hunt up the lost golf balls. Even at the very young age of seven or eight, Sally would caddy for players, sometime lugging two golf bags and their contents around a course.

One day, a customer for whom she caddied, ask Sally what she wanted for her birthday. She immediately told him her heart's desire was a pair of Mary Jane patent leather slippers, with a strap across the front and a button the sides.

He handed her two silver dollars and said, "Go ahead and buy yourself a pair." She ran right home to tell her mother about the generous man.

While her mother probably had better ideas for the money, a state militia couldn't have pried it loose from Sally. Her mother took her downtown to the Golden Rule Department Store to check out the Mary Jane slippers.

Next to the slippers were displayed what seemed like acres and acres of hair ribbons, which Sally really wanted. The Mary Jane slippers, however, would consumer her two silver dollars.

Sally and her sisters were forced to use elastic rubber bands to hold their hair in place.

While Sally stood transfixed in front of the hair ribbons, she noticed an elegant lady standing at her side. She asked, "Would you like to have some of those hair ribbons little girl?" she asked. Sally nodded enthusiastically.

The lady gave some sort of order to the salesgirl. She unwound yards and yards of every type of ribbon in every color. The lady then took the bag of ribbons from the clerk and set them in front of Sally, smiled sweetly, and then walked away.

I took the bag from the counter, stuffed it under my jacket and joined my mother.

Mother had often told me not to talk to strangers, but she seemed especially adamant about the lady in the ribbon department. Sally asked her mother, "Why didn't you want me to talk to that nice lady?"

"She was not a nice lady," my mother said. "She was a *painted* lady and I don't want you to ever talk to her again."

Sally kept her secret and the ribbons to herself for about two months. Then one day, she came home from the golf course and told her mother that the wife of a club member had given her the wonderful ribbons.

Sally's patent leather shoes were shown off proudly at the golf course. The only thing distracting from her new image came as she stooped over to pick up a golf ball. In full view of her customer, they were enabled to see my bloomers. Stretched across the seat were the words, "Happy Valley Flour".

Her mother had fashioned the rather undainty underthings out of the strongest and easiest to obtain material available.

During her poor days growing up, Sally's best friend was a Plymouth Rock chicken she called Emily. Sally had placed fourteen eggs under Emily, and she hatched eleven of them.

Sally's mother commented one day that the chickens were reaching the fryer stage. Sally had overheard the butcher at the shop tell a customer he was paying 75 cents each for fryers.

Sally devised a plan of action for her flock of fryers. She caught one and gently walked it to the butcher shop. She told the butcher she had to have the head and the feet for the dogs and cats at the farm.

Also, she told him, she needed the feathers for her mother to stuff into feather pillows.

With 75 cents in one hand and the head and feet of one of Emily's daughters in the other, Sally slinked back to the farm.

Sally spread the feathers over the chicken yard. She laid out the two feet and the head as well and waited for her mother to discover them.

"Do you think the dog did it?" her mother asked. Her mother inspected the dog's mouth for evidence of a chicken kill and found none. She then decided it was weasels.

One by one Sally abducted more chickens until only four or five were left. Her mother had finally deducted that it wasn't weasels at all, as the legs were cleanly cut.

Sally then quit asking the butcher for the feet.

The trouble with living in Baker City, Oregon, was that her father was not only an indifferent farmer, he was also an indifferent gambler and frequent drinker.

Sally's mother was a school teacher and had homesteaded three hundred and sixty acres of land in Burnt River, Oregon, near Baker City. Her father had done the same thing. Their homesteads lay adjacent to each other.

They decided to get married and my father rapidly lost everything. They then bought a house on one acre of land across from the golf links of Baker City.

This lasted longer than most other homesteads. Two more children, a brother and Sally were born there.

After 10 years in Baker City, Sally's father decided again to move. This time it was to a community called Sunnyslope, Oregon, outside of Baker City and on the Oregon Trail.

At age 14, Sally was called on to move to Santa Paula, California. Two of her aunts had died from an oil field fire. Sally was needed to care for her small cousins that were left motherless by the fire.

As the new girl in town, Sally came to the attention of a young oil-field worker named LeRoy Snyder. He was a nineteen-year old tall good-looking lad.

After a brief courtship, LeRoy asked Sally to marry him. To Sally, this meant she would never have to return to Medford, Oregon, and the drudgery that awaited her there.

"We took his mother's car and drove to Ventura where marriage laws were less stringent. I told the county clerk that I was 18."

When they retired to their bedroom on their wedding night, LeRoy went down the hall and came back dressed in cerise-colored pajamas. "He had a look on his face that "hogs have when the trough is full."

I sat on the edge of the bed with my hands in my lap. LeRoy suggested I take off my clothes.

"What for?" I asked, not knowing what the marriage bed was supposed to hold. "I was scared out of my wits."

In answer to LeRoy's pleadings to get undressed, I ran out of the house, leaving my few possessions behind.

She ran to the Pickwick Stage station to get a ticket home to Medford, Oregon. Sally had only a $5 bill. She was mortified when she learned a bus ticket to Medford would cost more than $30.

The answer to her problem came while she sat sobbing in the bus depot. A retired army sergeant saw her crying and offered to help. He was traveling to Portland and offered to take her back home. "He was a perfect gentleman the entire way."

LeRoy sent letter after letter trying to convince Sally to return. She left the letters unanswered. Finally, LeRoy gave up and had the marriage annulled.

Back in Medford, Sally worked at Wong's Café. One of the men she met was a guy much older than her, named Dan Goodan. Despite her mother's warnings that she just didn't like the man, Sally packed her straw suitcase with three jars of homemade strawberry jam and crept away from the house to meet Dan Goodan.

Where LeRoy talked, Dan acted. "I blissfully surrendered everything except my three jars of strawberry jam, before I realized we had forgotten something. We had forgotten to get married.

Dan merely laughed and said we could tie the knot in Colorado in his hometown to which we were headed.

Shortly after we had decided where to put the sofa in our house in Eaton, Colorado, the police came to the door and collected Dan. Dan worked for the Weiss Lumber Company as a bookkeeper.

He had given me a check written on the store's account. "I used the check to purchase an American Beauty Quick-Heating Electric Iron. The police sergeant was determined to wring a confession from me."

Trusting Dan was her first mistake. Sally ended up spending two years in Oregon State Prison for obtaining goods under false pretenses. The goods amounted to one American Beauty Quick-Heating Electric Iron.

In prison, Sally was assigned to the warden's house.

She was given a mountain of sewing to do and was also required to do some cooking. She remembered looking in the mirror every day and saying to herself, "A man got me into this, you dope, and from now on, don't take men seriously—just take them."

It was at this point that Sally vowed never to be broke again.

3

Her First Parlor House

While other parts of the country drank bathtub gin, San Francisco casually used the real stuff. Whiskey, Rum and other spirits were brought in from Canada.

San Francisco partied all night from the penthouses of Nob Hill to the Black Cat, Finocchios and on to Mona's lesbian joint that rivaled any upscale Parisian joint. Many of these partiers ended their evenings at Sally Stanford's, where champagne flowed all night.

Sally herself might whip up a batch of scrambled eggs. Sally's place became so famous a landmark that it was included on the city's several sightseeing tours.

One of Sally's first Parlor Houses was in the Russian Hill mansion once owned by Paul Verdier, proprietor of the elegant City of Paris department store.

A tour of the mansion revealed that each bedroom had a fireplace, causing Sally to remark "At no extra cost."

Sally commented on the people running the City of San Francisco. "They were a wonderful set of burglars. When I first came to town in 1923, they were stealing, but they were doing it with class and style."

It was at age 20 that she met Ernest Spagnoli. He was a San Francisco lawyer, who dropped by Sally's place in Ventura. It was the morning after she was visited by Probation Officers.

Ernest was trying to locate a woman by the name of Zelda Woodhayse. She had fleeced one of his clients. Sally invited him into the house for coffee.

He said he had to go to Los Angles for a court case. Sally needed to be in Los Angeles at the same time to fight a traffic ticket. Spagnoli also agreed to try her traffic case for free.

Ernest tried her case in court. When the judge set Sally's fine at $500 or 30 days in jail, Spagnoli brought out five crisp one-hundred-dollar bills and paid her bail. He told the judge he would appeal the case. He did appeal and won.

Sally stayed in Los Angeles for three days, wined and dined by Spagnoli. As they drove back to Santa Barbara the next day, he did a strange thing.

He said, "You're a pretty nice kid, I like you—let's get married."

One of the most flagrant of the city hall group was Mayor Jimmy Rolph, also known as "Sunny Jim". At one time in Rolph's colorful career, he was asked to make a statement about prostitution.

His reply was: "Leave it alone."

The Tenderloin was teeming with prosperity. Most French restaurants had private rooms.

A curious coincidence occurred during Jimmy Rolph's tenure as mayor. Statistics on rape crimes were the lowest per capita that they had ever been.

This pernicious form of mischief in San Francisco lasted for more than 30 years. "Nothing lasts that long unless the people are willing that it should," Sally said.

At one point, Sally went to her husband Ernest and suggested they adopt a child. Sally made the arrangement with a woman that had too many children to handle. She took the little fellow home to love and cuddle.

At this same time, Sally's husband Ernest became heir to a sizeable fortune. His sister, who disliked Sally, suggested to him that an adopted child could become heir to his fortune.

"We can solve the whole thing very easily," Sally said. "Ernest can keep the money and I'll take the child."

They decided to leave each other while there was still a good deal of respect left. With the money she had left over from her Ventura enterprise, Sally bought a little hotel at 693 O'Farrell Street.

She kept her car in the name of Marcia Wells in case the hotel went under.

The fact that Sally was accused of being a madam hung heavy on her head and her reputation. It also put a wall between her and her husband Ernest Spagnoli and his family.

She realized she couldn't use the name Marcia Spagnoli without embarrassing Ernest. She was equally sure she wasn't going to be Marcia Busby again.

"It happened on the weekend of the University of California and Stanford football faceoff. She noticed the headline in the newspaper: STANFORD BEATS CALIFORNIA. She was all for Stanford and suddenly, she knew she had a new name.

San Francisco was the last major city in the United States where commercial society and vice were frank and open commodities.

Spider Kelly's at Mason and Ellis had entertainment that would nowadays be playing in Las Vegas. Bones Remmer's Menlo Park Club on Eddy Street and the Kingston and Chad Milligan's drew the top gamblers in the country.

In her book, *The Lady of the House*", Sally wrote that the French restaurants, particularly, such as *Germaine's, Pierre's, The Poodle Dog*, and *Blanco's* were as famous for their rooms upstairs as for their sauces on their restaurant menus.

The Poodle Dog boasted an elevator to allow its girls quick access to the rooms upstairs. Blanco's had an even larger elevator to carry a greater number of ladies to their upstairs destinations.

When the Reverend Paul Smith, a protestant minister was approached and solicited by one of the street lady's, he gave a walloping sermon about the incident at his Sunday church meeting.

Because of the sermon, the police felt they should act. They suspended all activity on the block in question as well as three adjacent blocks.

Reverend Smith was overwhelmed by the large congregation that appeared in his church the next Sunday. Most of the faces glaring at him were more furious than rapt.

Every woman that had been thrown out of work because of Reverend Smith's complaint was present. Their spokesperson was an articulate woman named Reggie Gamble.

She began speaking without an invitation to do so. She asked what the good people of the church and their shepherd were going to do about some two hundred women from whom their daily bread had been snatched.

The Reverend Smith suggested that everything would come out o.k. because of the love and faith of the congregation.

The unemployed ladies were strangely silent. They literally decided to become neighbors of the church. They moved into every dwelling adjoining the church, and they weren't there to do housework.

Sally Stanford decided to move her bordello to 610 Leavenworth Street.

"I want to say here and now that at no time, did I ever knowingly hire a non-professional to work for me. I only wanted girls who knew what they were doing, and I discouraged all amateurs from getting into the business."

Sally also decided that her "house" would have to be the best in the world. She decorated it with the best materials from the finest furniture stores. She instructed a maid to remain at the front door and to shut the door in the face of any customer who wasn't gentleman enough to make known his wants in words of more than four letters.

The Mayor of San Francisco, Sunny Jim Rolph, began entertaining politicians at Sally's house.

While Sally dropped out of school in the third grade, she would read virtually everything she could get her hands on. She developed her own education.

4

Famous Stars
Were Banned

If you couldn't be a gentleman in one of Sally's Bawdy Houses, you might easily be banned. This happened to some of the rich and famous as well ordinary men.

One such person that got banned was Humphrey Bogart. Sally recalls that Bogart was a drunken boor who badgered, insulted and abused Sally's employees.

"We finally had to eighty-six him. He simply had no class."

On the other hand, she found Errol Flynn to be sweet. "He was the only customer I ever had that tested all of the talent, including both shifts, twice."

Flynn was noted for entertaining leading ladies, other men's wives, and a coterie of young ladies still eligible for Girl Scout badges.

In 1942, a group of Errol Flynn's friends pulled a most notorious prank on him. After spending hours drowning their sorrows over the death of their friend John Barrymore, three of the mourners bribed the undertaker and headed back to Flynn's house with Barrymore's body.

They propped the body up in a chair and waited for Flynn to arrive after a late-night date.

Flynn screamed upon seeing the body and hid in an oleander bush on the patio. He recovered quickly and poured drinks for his friends but refused to help them return the body.

A combination of accident and luck brought Flynn to Hollywood. It was after a film producer saw him on an Australian beach.

Sally Stanford railed against the post war migration of Midwesterners to California. "They brought their Bible Belt morality with them and tried to suppress the city's free life style.

They voted, like the people they were, for purity and started the destruction of the spirit of the colorful city that had fascinated them. These are the people who called the town 'Frisco'."

Sally didn't hesitate to take on other people of importance, including the Nob Hill class.

"Perhaps the real sinners were the illustrious robber barons who occupied the other houses on Nob Hill.

Among them was Leland Stanford himself. Stanford was one of the Big Four who built the Central Pacific Railroad and held the entire economy in their monopolistic grip."

She noted that the Big Four built the railroads with cheap Chinese labor, charged exorbitant freight rates and with false promises, lured thousands of migrant farmers west.

5

Girl's Home
Away from Home

Sally's house at 610 Leavenworth was a home away from home to many lonesome characters.

"We prospered," Sally Stanford said, "but there were a lot of things I had to learn, and I learned them the hard way. I found out that fully fifty percent of the girls who became prostitutes were 100 percent foolish."

Among the other half were some of the cleverest, most resourceful females I'd ever encountered.

Sally found one problem with her girls was the pimps that virtually controlled them. "The women need these leeches like a turtle needs music lessons, she harped." Sooner or later a girl will show up with a glib male who begins to mastermind her career.

33

He will ultimately leave her at precisely the point where she is at the lowest ebb of her life.

She will be lucky if he leaves her with enough money for cyanide and carfare to the morgue.

"Why these women feel they need these leeches is beyond me. Whatever the cause for the prevalence of pimpery, it is stubbornly there."

She said she learned a lot about men from my customers at 610 Leavenworth Street. "I learned to get the money first. Many men, especially those with a few drinks, tended to be roguish and amused at the idea of not paying as soon as they zipped up."

Sally said she learned that men came to her establishment not just for sex but for a lot of other reasons. These included talking about their troubles, their wives' infidelities, to sleep off a drunk, or to find any new wrinkles in the sex game.

"I thought I had learned my lesson from life, but I must have not, because I fell in love again. This trip to the alter was with a good looking fellow by the name of Lou Rapp. This marriage lasted thirteen years."

6

The Mayor
Becomes A Customer

Mayor Sunny Jim Rolph became a customer, although not a guest of the house. The mayor sent his secretary to make the arrangements. The mayor was not the kind to bring his personal business to a house of prostitution.

Mayor Rolph did a lot of entertaining. For one such event his guests were all men. The mayor leased a Caucasian geisha house at 699 Sanchez Street. The mayor's secretary said three bright, good natured and able-bodied young ladies were needed for the event.

Sunny Jim charmed his constituents. Even as governor in 1931, he owned the Pleasure Den, a whorehouse at 21st and Sanchez. On his way to work in his limousine, he was famous for picking up pedestrians along the street and driving them to their destination. When we entered my place, he said, "So you're Sally Stanford. You're a pretty one."

Sally weighed a scant 110 pounds and wore a stunning suit in two shades of blue. She also had an ostrich feather in her hat.

Sunny Jim sat down and immediately started negotiations. "I smiled and pointed out to him that I was the madam and not the merchandise," Sally recalled.

He asked Sally into his office. "Keep them clean and pretty, Sally. Don't ever lose your class. Do things with class and style, and you'll always have the respect even of those who are against you, even the Bible-bangers."

Sally said her meeting with Sunny Jim Rolph was the beginning of a long and fine friendship with the mayor.

One day, after he ducked his driver, he called her from the grill of the Whitcomb Hotel and suggested she drop over. Jimmy was feeling pretty low and was hung over.

It seems his wife Annie had put a detective on him and found several transgressions. "Something had to be done or his candidacy for governor was going to be as a bachelor.

When she next saw Sunny Jim, he had been elected Governor of California.

He took time out from interviewing a long list of people wanting to see him to invite Sally into his office.

When he died, Sally closed the office for the day and sent the largest floral display she could find. She did not put a card with the display. "I didn't want to blow his class."

7

Sally Liked Her Diamonds

The illustrious Sally liked her stylish clothes. But she liked diamonds even more. She noted that her choice of clothing was soon attracting more attention than did her profession.

"Flamboyant clothes, the stereotype of a madam, never attracted me, she said. I do like to make an entrance. I think every woman does."

Sally was most fond of her diamond collection. "Diamonds, I go for. I could always hock them in my old age if things got rough. You never know when that problem might pop up its ugly head as you move through life."

She noted that even on her ranch, diamonds set off her cotton blouses and blue jeans. Diamonds were a great source of morale and far more stable than the Treasury Department's green stationery.

Sally began getting around more socially, meeting many of her colleagues in the prostitution business. "I usually took along several of my prettiest girls as it was good advertising.

She recalled one San Francisco madam who was shaped like a butterball. "If she had fallen, she would still be rolling," she laughed.

At her house at Sixth and Minna, the obese madam was made famous for allowing a customer another round with the same lady when the first tryst was unsatisfactory.

Her credo was, "If at first you don't succeed, come, come again."

Another madam on her visitation list was Lorraine Fontaine. Lorraine was found dead one night in her empty, girl-less house. All the girls had fled as no one wanted to indulge in lengthy conversations with investigating authorities.

Another madam recalled to memory by Sally was "Immaculate Maggie", so called by newspapermen because she retired after 20 years without a single pinch.

One or two of the San Francisco madams actually looked like madams. Most looked like young society matrons.

"Of them all," Sally said, "I liked Mabel Malotte best. Mabel was a pro, a wonderful little woman.

She had more class in her little finge than all of the people who finally cooperated in her crucifixion. "For years, Mabel staged a high-voltage love affair with a handsome policeman. Theirs was a Frankie and Johnnie affair, a flame of passion that was unquenchable. He was supposed to be able to take care of matters when problems arose."

When trouble fell for Mabel from the police department, her man was looking the other way. Mabel, Sally said, also handled the situation badly. She was sentenced to Corona for perjury and other offenses.

"Uncle Sam was waiting for her when she came out with a whole mess of other trouble, effective the day of her release. I kept in touch with her and we planned ways for her to fight off the nightmare and come back to some sort of life. Then she got cancer."

Mabel fought off the cancer and stayed alive until she was released. She finally collapsed in the Greyhound Bus Terminal while trying to reach the Ladies' Room.

When she recovered, she was a shell of a woman. She was in the same hospital Sally was in while recovering from a heart attack. We were on the same floor and I would visit her.

"She told me how her attorneys had taken all of her money."

Mabel reminded me of a pact we had made years earlier that if one of us died before the other we would provide a fine funeral.

On the day before Christmas in 1958, her private nurse came into my room and told me that my friend Mabel was dead. I immediately reach for the phone and called Halstead's Funeral Parlor, asking them to pick up Mabel's remains.

Mabel had left her entire estate to Victor Herbert who wasn't around when Lady Luck walked out on Mabel. Victor had died thirteen days before Mabel.

8

The Protection Racket

It was Sally's belief that the downfall of the Tenderloin District came at the hands of a woman from Hawaii.

So-called Princess Alice Kamokila Campbell was the wealthy daughter of a Hawaiian sugar planter. She had a son called Pineapple McFarland.

Princess Alice wanted to star in her own nightclub. She opened her club at a vacant Methodist Church at Bush and Jones streets. She called it *Club Kamokila.*

The newly-arrived Hawaiian princess opened a real can of worms for the Tenderloin District. She called the police department and asked to be connected to the man who collected "protection money".

The flabbergasted policeman who answered the call referred it to the Chief of Police, William J. Quinn. The Kamokila Club was raided and carried on page one of all newspapers.

The princess packed up her belongings and headed back to Hawaii.

Still, the town was filled with talk about "protection". This sent a warning chill up Sally's spine. Princess Alice had "tossed dirt into the punch bowl."

The town was filled with talk about protection. "My personal warning system told me there would be a big shake-up," Sally wrote in her book. "I had never paid off. I don't believe in it, but you don't make friends with the protection by withholding your dues."

Newspapers were of the opinion that San Francisco faced the end of a wide-open town as it was known. It seemed that everyone was checking on someone.

An employee of the Internal Revenue Service told a Mill Valley luncheon club that a certain San Francisco policeman was being investigated for having banked over one hundred thousand dollars from his annual salary of $7,000.

There was also the rumor that certain madams were being investigated for listing graft payoffs as business expenses. It was rumored that a professional "peeper" would be looking into these charges.

Sally said, "I had a policeman friend that told me to be on the lookout for a large-shouldered, square-jawed joker who would probably call and ask questions other than those a madam might expect from a client."

Several days later, a policeman named Frank Lucey, who often came by for coffee, told me, "You're going to have to close, Sally. It might be a good idea to take a little vacation, you and the girls. Reno's very nice this time of year."

I asked, "Do you just mean my business?"

"No, I mean everyone this side of the dry goods business. The heat is on."

He told me that the Grand Jury had hired Edwin Atherton, a former FBI man as a professional peeper. Even before he came out with his famous "Atherton Report", things were going in a tailspin.

When the report came out, it was 70 pages long. It named and located every brothel in town. Every girl on every staff, plus her measurements, and her preference in disinfectants were listed.

One day, when it was too early for business, Sally had a visitor. It was the dreaded Edwin Atherton, the Grand Jury peepster who wrote the Atherton report.

I was counting the receipts from the day before. Gloria, the black maid who handled the laundry for the house, was checking the towel supply. Gloria answered the doorbell. She came to me and said, "This man I ain't never seen before. He say he have a friend."

I stuffed the money receipts I was counting into the bottom of a smoking stand. I put the records under a cushion on the settee.

"When the big, large-shouldered, square-jawed joker came in, I knew I was face-to-face with brother Atherton."

He handed Sally a card. She asked, "Why in the world would you want to talk to the proprietor of a quiet little place for rented rooms?"

"Come on Sally, everyone knows that you run a good, clean, sensible house of prostitution. We can talk, Sally, I'm not interested in giving you a bad time."

The melody is always the same, and Sally knew the lyrics. He would tell her that nothing would happen to her, but in her own mind she knew she might have to go to work folding sheets in a laundry.

Unfortunately, Gloria, the maid, came through the room carrying about ninety towels over her arms. Atherton eyed the towels. "We take a lot of baths," Sally told him.

She ushered Atherton to the door, saying she would give a lot of thought to what he had said. He replied, "Don't call us, we'll call you."

Sally had working establishments at 837 Geary Street, 929 Bush Street, and an Oriental establishment at 1224 Stockton Street in Chinatown and another on Taylor Street.

Her place on Taylor Street was adjacent to the Japanese Consulate. One evening, a delegation of policemen arrived.

While they were talking with the maid, three working girls departed by the rear fire escape. The ladies summoned a cab and sped off to the Japanese Consulate. The bewildered policemen watched this action goggle-eyed.

Sally got a bit of free advertising at her Chinatown house. When she would hire a new girl, the word was spread fast and furious.

Fliers with Chinese lettering appeared on every telephone pole and building in the area, noting that "SALLY'S GOT A NEW GIRL". No one could read it except for the wily Orientals as it was written in Chinese.

9

Working in A Brothel

Madam Sally voiced her opinion about white slavery. "Personally, I never met a white slave in my life. If captive famales were sold, drugged, or slugged into prostitution, I never knew the case."

A far more common practice that annoyed Sally was the arrival of unsuitable women to work in her brothels.

"Most of them were clearly unfit to do so. They were either too dull, too plain, too young or completely without experince," Sally said in her book, *"The Lady of the House"*.

She continued, "I sent most of them on their way with advice to keep out of the business. "I had no use for the unprofessionals. They were bad for business in the same fashion as an untrained, inexperienced court reporter who could mess up the records. A good girl needs a lot more than standard equipment."

The greatest number who rang Sally's doorbell were women who simply wanted to be prostitutes. They simply wanted to have intercourse with men for money.

There were others who envisioned the illicit activity as glamorous. A large number of applicants were neurotic, who had marriages or love affairs that soured .

A lot of women who showed up at Sally's door had a desire to become glamorous queens of the red-light district. Also, Sally found, every size, shape and color of dope addict wanted into the profession.

The narcotics habit was expensive, costing fifty to seventy five dollars a day during that period. "I learned years ago to recognize hopheads immediately. They are all messed up and they foul up the business and keep you in trouble constantly. I never knowingly put one to work."

Most of the drug addicted women had not only themselves to support but the support of their pimp as well.

Sally said one narcotics addict did slip by her. She was an educated girl whose youthful freshness would have deceived the narcotics bureau of the FBI. She took her money and I never saw her again. "I learned the bitter truth when newspapers published her picture after she was found dead from an overdose of heroin."

Madam Sally decided to abandon the low rent district of the Tenderloin and concentrate on the more elegant neighborhoods of San Francisco.

She decided to follow San Francisco Mayor Jim Rolph's advice and do everything with "Style and Class".

She headed for Nob Hill, Russian Hill and the Pacific Heights where the carpets are thicker.

10

Sally Moves Uptown

When Sally decided to go upscale, she considered a house at 1001 Vallejo Street. It was built by Robert Hanford for his fourth wife. Architects had been given carte blanche in its design.

She finally selected a mansion at 1144 Pine Street. Both houses were spectacular and both were fortresses. It was impossible for anyone to enter unless they were welcomed by Sally or her employees.

In the Pine Street house, every room and every floor was different. One floor was designed as a hunting lodge. There were also Oriental, Italian, French Provincial, and Venetian Renaissance rooms.

The rooms were decorated with the finest antiques. Soft music was piped throughout the house. Fine food and vintage wines were served throughout the day.

"We were concerned only with the kind of men who were not concerned about the price tags."

Thirty to fifty dollars was the normal fee for a half hour of a girl's time. Many guests paid from two hundred-fifty to five-hundred dollars for hospitality. The higher rates included liquor and food."

When gentlemen arrived, they were greeted by a host or hostess who satisfied themselves that the guest was neither a policeman nor a pauper. Sally's Chinese butler, Wong Hee, knew every cop in the city. He also served the drinks.

The conversation was always good. Sally never allowed her girls to tell a dirty story to her guests. The clientele who came to her place resented such stories, Sally felt.

"As for me, I was as removed from any of the surface amenities of prostitution as if I were a housemother at Vassar."

I chose the girls with equal care. Nearly all of them were from out of town. Many of them were former showgirls or models.

"No merchant was more meticulous about his wares than I was about mine," said Sally. "Each candidate had the services of my medical doctor, my hairdresser and my dressmaker."

Sally was generous, giving her girls 60 percent of their take. Even though she preached against girls having pimps, invariably some would show up with a black eye and a request for an advance.

Although Sally sought high class clients, it didn't always work out. Some just had their problems.

For instance, one of the town's most eligible bachelors exhibited problems with weak kidneys.

When he was in his cups, he would go into any available vase, coal bucket, umbrella stand, champagne cooler, or upended crate.

When this happened, my first warning would be from the screams of the girls to the effect that "He's at it again."

In one case it was the furious shouts of another gentleman whose hundred dollar Stetson was receiving the urinal treatment.

Another sometimes difficult guest was actually well-liked by the girls. If he had been drinking, he had a difficult time paying his bill after he had indulged in a sexual encounter.

Sally had a special rule for him. She had the hostess pick up his shoes and hide them early in each visit. One night, there was a raid by cops, although they never got beyond the front door.

The girls and the guests were herded out the back door. Among them was the guest whose shoes had been hidden. The man went home barefooted.

It's hard to love your neighbor, especially when the neighbor blows the whistle on you.

It was in my Russian Hill house that a new matron had moved in a few doors from my house. She decided to give a welcome party for her neighbors. She tucked invitations under each door.

I said to my girls, "Well, let's go. It may be a lark."

As her party was in full swing, Sally and her girls arrived and was treated like royalty.

Word was dropped that Sally's stable of fillies were getting most of the male guests' attention.

The hostess disappeared and the party died of its own volition.

One day, Sally got a visitor in the form of police Captain Emmett Moore of Central Station. He kindly informed Sally that a lot of complaints about her presence on Russian Hill were going to the Police Chief.

Sally said, "I decided to move to another deluxe address where the neighbors had more to do than peep through their draperies and put a stopwatch on the visits of my guests."

It was in 1941 that Sally bought the house at 1144 Pine Street. She remained at that location until 1948, when she retired from the prositution business.

"The house could not have been more perfect if I had designed it myself," she said. It was designed by New York architect Stanford White. The only entry was through a wrought iron gate which could have kept out a regiment of marines.

It was two blocks from the fashionable Fairmont and Mark Hopkins hotels and a short walk from the St. Francis and Sir Francis Drake hotels.

Sally furnished the house with the best and launched it with a masked ball. No one ever entered without invitation.

San Francisco columnist Herb Caen contended that Sally's House on Pine Street claimed the United Nations was formed there because so many delegates convened there.

One day, Sally drove to the beach, taking some of her girls with her.

While there, a middle-aged matron approached Sally, saying, "I've never seen such lovely and charming girls. You must be running a finishing school for such delightful debutantes."

Sally said, "Something like that," moving toward her car.

The woman followed, begging a ride into town. During the ride, she told the group that she specialized in teaching French literature, proper English, and a course in ettiquette.

"Do keep me in mind," she told Sally.

The girls howled when the woman finally departed the car.

11

The Ugly Applicant

One eager applicant was one of the ugliest women in the world. This creature was fashioned with such utmost consistency that every part of her competed with the rest in homeliness.

Her earnestness and determination to work even for free moved me, said Sally. "I called in my staff to decide what to do with her. When I asked her to strip, as I do with all my new employees, the rest of her was equally consistent with her face."

This creature had a fervent yearning to share, so we tried. In less time than it takes to tell this story she became the toast of the house.

"This babe was so devoted to her work, so cooperative and so violent in the ecstasy department she produced in my guests, she got all the business.

The other girls began complaining until I suggested that she set herself up and keep the profits.

You simply can't tell by the wrapping. Some real beauties have proved to be real duds.

One rule strictly enforced by Sally was that neither of the iron doors of the house were to be opened after normal hours. One night after a busy night, everyone was tired and deserved some rest.

Sally had given orders to her staff that neither the door nor the telephone should be answered.

Sally explained she had just gotten into her chiffon nighty, put her hair up in curlers, when the front buzzer rang. She thought she would check it out herself.

It was a valuable oil painting and the delivery boy had simply stuck it through the iron bars of the front gate and departed. A draft of wind slammed the door shut behind Sally.

She was trapped in her own vestibule in her nightgown. Ring and knock as she might, nobody answered her calling.

"I stopped one pleasant looking gentleman and asked him to phone the house number. I heard the phone ringing off the wall, but no one answered.

Finally, one of the girls decided to leave and opened the inner door to let herself out. "I stamped upstairs, disgruntled and furious," Sally recalled.

Then, the phone rang wildly. I answered it and a pleasant male voice said, "Lady, will you open your inner door as there's some broad in your vestibule that can't get in."

12

Out to Get Sally

In her book, "*The Lady of the House*", Sally writes about one police detective's determination to "get Sally Stanford" at all costs. The man in question was Sergeant John Dyer.

He became so intense in his attempt to bring her down that he spent both his own money and his own time on the project.

Two gentlemen, a Mr. Grossman and a Mr. Smith, showed up at my establishment one afternoon, wanting girls, Sally says.

"My premonition gong began to chime. I had my houseman Wong Hee usher them into a room equipped with two-way communication. In short, the room was bugged."

Sally talked with them for a while and then asked for their identification.

Mr. Grossman was supposedly a drapery goods salesman and carried a case of handsome fabrics. He presented Mr. Smith as an old friend from out of town.

Wong Hee, was instructed to served them drinks. He was also told to refuse to take their money. Grossman kept trying to tuck a few bills in Wong's pocket, without success.

When Sally listened in on the men's conversations, Grossman, said, "She's in the bag." His companion, Smith said, "I don't know. I think she's giving us the 'oakie doakie'."

"Don't you believe it," Grossman said. "It was these drapery samples that did it. She figures she's conning me out some free material. Women forget everything else when there's a chance of getting something for free. We're in solid. Johnny will love it."

Sally went to the window and spotted their police car parked at the end of the street across the way. In it was her old nemesis Sergeant John Dyer.

Wong Hee whispered in my ear, "Mr. Glossman, he poleeseman. I see him all the time on Turk Street. One time I see him 'allest' lady; big sheet heel, Mr. Glossman, but I think he have othah name."

"I think so too, Wong, but give him another drink, smile like you love him forever, don't take a dime, and I'll get the girls on their way."

Sally returned to the men, saying, "All the secretaries are gone for the day."

"Secretaries!" Grossman shouted.

"Yes, you wanted to give some dictation, didn't you? We've got the best secretarial service in town."

"Frigged, after all this trouble," Smith said. "I told you so, you smart bastard."

Outside the window, Sally noticed her girls were being arrested. She was at the Hall of Justice with a bail bondsman almost before the girls arrived. Within the hour the girls were dismissed. They had been booked as vagrants.

A few weeks later, Jackson, her aide, said Santa Claus may be a little early this year. He pointed to a man on the roof of the house next door. He was making the narrow jump to the roof of my house.

"I phoned the Central Station and reported a prowler. I joined the officers in the street when they arrived.

They ordered the man down from my roof. When I recognized that it was John Dyer, I said, take him away. I won't prefer charges."

13

United Nations Delegates Loved Sally's

Forty-six chapters of the United Nations converged on San Francisco for a conference in 1945. They spent about as much time at Sally's emporiums as they did at the conference itself.

Foreign diplomats availed themselves of everything Sally's had to offer, including her mattress sports. Some never bothered to leave.

The press even reported that the major action of the United Nations delegates was taking place at Sally's. While Russian, Chinese, Czech, English, Norwegian and Mexican delegates felt much at home, it was the Arabians, Hindus, Egyptians and Pakistani that grabbed the attention.

One night, an order came in from the desert sheiks, saying they wanted several girls. The order stipulated, "No Jewish Girls".

The handwriting of Sally's hostess, Rosanna, was not always easy to decipher. It appeared she had written 110 girls in such a way to make it appear they wanted 110 Jewish girls, when in fact the order stipulated no Jewish girls.

When I picked up the notepad, I hit the telephone, calling even my competition, to solicit 110 Jewish girls. I rounded up twenty-five and figured we could run them in shifts and make it seem like 110.

The men arranged themselves in groups around the salon until it looked like a Cecil B. De Mille production. "I had supplied each of the girls with a mezuzah to support her Jewish appearance."

One tribal chieftain called me aside and asked what the things were the girls kept waving at us. I hurriedly explained that they were a wonderful American contraceptive.

My phone, at one time, rang in the odd hours with the most cultured and masculine voice. He would say things, however, that were completely vile and incredible.

Sally said she had the telephone company trace the calls.

They were traced to the most handsome, best-mannered, and outstanding member of a solidly elite social San Francisco family.

"He was frightened silly by his entrapment," said Sally. I asked authorities to tell him if he continued such calls that his family would be notified."

This stopped the calls as far as my phone was concerned.

One of my girls, Thelma, was a poetry reader who also loved dogs.

She was forever bringing in a stray she had found or rescued from the dog pound. "Please, Sally, just for a few days until I can find it a home." I was a pushover because I, too, loved pets.

The idea, however, struck me strange.

"Imagine, dogs in a cathouse."

14

Sally's Personal Loves

People are always curious about Sally's personal sexual encounters. Sally admits to being married several times. "It sure as hell wasn't for money."

"Love is not all fire, sex and passion," Sally wrote in her autobiography, *The Lady of the House*". Those fires, she explained, flare up, go off like a sky rocket, and fall like a clinker to the bottom of the grate."

She said her husband, Lou Rapp, was both handsome and charming. He was also compulsively neat. "Lou was a cleaner-upper with fervor! I never knew whether he had taken the brass hinges off the doors, polished them and forgotten to screw them back on firmly.

One time, Sally said, Lou arranged the parlor of their home with new upholstered sofas. He was so proud of his work that he got carried away.

"He stretched ribbon across the front of the sofas to prevent anyone from sitting in them. It was like the DeYoung Museum."

Sally characterized her marriage to husband Bob Gump, a department store heir, as most improbable. "For a Gump to marry Sally Stanford was rather improbable to the rest of the world."

Bob Gump was something of a curio, himself, said Sally. "I suspect it was not the happiest moment for Bob's family to learn they had annexed me as a shiksa (a disparaging term for a non-Jewish woman)."

Our wedding supper turned out to be a very lively social event. Bob was overcome with emotion and too much to drink. Someone then set fire to the john.

Firemen were called and were furious because illegally parked cars blocked their access to the fire hydrants. They called the cops and he police arrived and distributed tickets like confetti. Guests were furious. It was a very gay and dizzy omen.

Bob once told me about his mother, Mabel Gump, counseling both him and his brother Dick on the facts of life. The boys were only 11 or 12 years old at the time.

After she had told the boys all that she considered proper for their age, she asked her husband, A.L. Gump, to advise them further.

"Abe," she told her husband, "I've told them all I could about the facts of life. Now you must elaborate on what I've said."

Bob's father agreed to do so on Saturday. As they walked downhill toward the synagogue, the father stopped suddenly. "Boys," he said, "Don't go with whores."

A newspaper columnist noted in his column one day that two ladies walked by Gump's store one day. One of them commented to the other one. "There's the famous Gump's. They are getting very prominent here, aren't they?"

"Yes, yes, indeed, replied her friend. "Why one of them recently married into the Stanford Clan."

Another Gump story reported by Sally Stanford, concerned another famous madam, Dodie Valencia.

Gump senior was apparently having financial trouble with his famous store. Dodie came into the store one day and admired a painting priced at $16,000. She said she would have to think about it.

When she later heard the news that Gump's may have to close their doors, Dodie took cash to the store and purchased the painting.

Bob Gump and I separated two years later.

Next, Bob Kenna came into my life. He was the middleman in Sally's collection of husbands.

Kenna was strictly a ladies' man. "When it looked like my bookkeeper was too close to my husband and my accounts, I let them both go", said Sally.

Practically all my husbands are still friends of mine, Sally said.

On one New Year's Eve, I was unmarried at the time. The name of one of my ex-husbands came to mind. I dialed his number and received no answer.

Sally drove to his apartment. The apartment was dark, and no one answered the doorbell. Feeling something was terribly wrong, Sally went to the building manager. She refused to open my ex-husband's door without the permission of the tenant.

"For the first time in a long time, I called the police," said Sally. When the cops arrived they found nothing wrong. They told Sally the man inside was simply sleeping.

This disturbed Sally even more.

"Listen," she told the rookie cops, "that ex-husband of mine was the most annoying light sleeper I've ever known." She insisted they go back into the apartment.

Sally turned on the bedroom light and saw at the foot of the bed an empty cardboard box. It had once been full of sleeping pills.

"Can't you see this man is dying," Sally told the cops. They immediately called an ambulance.

As they carted the body away, one of the cops turned to Sally and said, "I never believed in women's tuition before."

Her ex-husband pulled out of his self-induced coma. Sally returned home to her own world again.

15

The Booker T Society

The Booker T Society was conceived, invented and swung into action by Red Clark. He was the International News Service reporter on the police beat at the Hall of Justice.

Red arrived at his office broke, hung over and newsless.

He sat there at his desk waiting for inspiration. He picked up his phone and dialed the Regal Amber Brewery. He asked for the superintendent.

"This is the press room at the Hall of Justice," he told the superintendent. "When does the beer arrive.?"

"Who ordered the beer? Who's going to pay for it?"
"Pay! This is the *press*! This is a citywide celebration to be celebrated by dignitaries, prominent citizens, and maybe even your own boss, don't you know what day this is?"

When the superintendent drew a blank, Red spied a calendar with a list of all holidays. "This is the birthday of Booker T Washington, a pioneer Negro educator."

The superintendent said he would send the beer right over.

Red Clark next negotiated with Max Sobel's wholesale liquor firm, the Langendorf Bakery, and three delicatessens in the Tenderloin.

Since Red had promised dignitaries, he called out-of-work newsmen and invited them and their girls; he extended invitations to his own creditors, including his tailor, who muttered about Red putting something down on his newest set of threads.

He contacted Supervisor Dewey Mead who could make a speech at the drop of a hat, bookmaker Paul Bouquet Cohen, and Painless Parker, the millionaire chain dentist. Naturally, Sally Stanford was an invited guest.

The goodies and beer showed up promptly along with judges, gamblers, cops, attorneys and county jail matrons. They were all asking in their private groups, "Where is this guy, Booker T Washington?"

Booker T Washington became a tradition in the newspaper world of San Francisco and Red Clark became its high priest.

Sally wrote in her book that as a charter member of the Booker T Washington club she continued to participate each year.

In one celebration, a squad of ladies arrived from the Booker T Washington auxiliary of one of the Negro Churches. Covered dishes, spareribs, berry pies and their minister arrived with them.

A few years later the Booker T Washington society suspended its meetings.

16

Sally's Unusual Courtroom Drama

One of Sally's saddest experiences came at the hands of her brother Merle, second oldest of her brothers. Merle worked on a dairy farm milking and tending cows.

He became infatuated with the daughter of the owner of the dairy farm.

One day, Sally was visited at her Bush Street house by two men from the Bureau of Missing Persons. Their first question to Sally was whether she knew Merle.

She replied yes and asked why they needed to know.

One of the men told her that her brother was wanted for kidnapping of a young girl from Livingston.

Sally narrowly missed connecting with her brother when she searched the hotels the next day. However, the missing girl's mother and an aunt called on Sally the next day.

They didn't have any luggage. They went into detail about how poor they were.

I was remodeling my Bush Street house, but I offered them a room upstairs between a concrete wall and the working contractors.

Sally asked if they would like to talk to the chief of the missing persons bureau. They quickly replied no. Sally asked if there was something she could do.

"They wanted to go to the World's Fair Exposition,", she said. They even asked her if should wanted to go with them. "No, I can't think of doing anything like that at a time like this," Sally answered.

Sally learned later that the ladies were put up to their shenanigans by the Merced County district attorney. The Merced district attorney had visited the home of Sally's housekeeper. While she was shocked about hearing about Merle, she told the D.A. that she knew nothing about Merle and his activities.

The D.A. and a special prosecutor next met with San Francisco's Chief of Police, asking for the arrest of Sally Stanford.

When Sally looked out of her bedroom window on Bush Street the next morning, she saw cops running all about her place. "Rosanna (Sally's assistant) and Sally were both arrested on charges of a child-stealing plot with my brother.

Sally and Rosanna were taken to county jail. The toughest judge on the bench heard their lawyer's plea for release. He refused to let them go.

Our bail was $500 each, but at 6 a.m., both Sally and Rosanna were hustled off to Livingston in Merced County. By then they were safely incarcerated there. The bail had jumped to $25,000.

Then, a 54-count information sheet was issued charging both Sally and Rosanna with a host of offenses. These included everything from pandering, running a disorderly house, kidnapping, white slavery, and others.

These charges were used to get the courts to raise the bail to $100,000 cash or $200,000 by bond.

Sally's attorney went to court and got the bail reduced to $20,000 cash, or $40,000 by bond, which Sally made herself. It was not, however, before she and Rosanna spent 16 days in jail.

"These were 16 of the most stinking days I've ever spent anywhere," Sally said. "It was a filthy hole, crawling with lice and filth, and the first breakfast was a bowl of prunes. I counted several bugs in that bowl."

The only person who was able to separate the facts in the case, Sally said, was Judge Hal Shaeffer.

The judge separated the case of her brother Merle from the case of Sally and Rosanna.

Whiling sitting in jail Sally kept thinking that she knew the matron who visited every day. The connection finally came to her. She asked the matron, "Did you ever know the former coroner of Merced County?"

"Why yes. I'm his widow."

Sally then remembered. "My former husband Ernest Spagnoli defended your brother-in-law in Santa Rosa for murder of his mother-in-law." He was found not guilty by reason of insanity.

Sally declined attempts by Merced County attorneys to defend her. Instead, she sought an old San Francisco attorney friend by the name of Leo Friedman.

Sally said, "We subpoenaed everybody. The only ones who didn't show up were the Salvation Army."

A county clerk approached Sally asking if some of the witnesses waiting to testify couldn't go home? "Are you going to use all of these witnesses? Can't some of them go home? They are a great expense to the county, you know."

Sally promptly answered, "I don't give a damn about the county's expense. You don't think that bevy of barristers in there are working for nothing do you? When I go home, they go home."

When the aunt and mother of the missing girl appeared in court, they testified that Sally and Rosanna tried to hypnotize them by locking them in their apartment and not letting them go.

80

The case fell apart by the weight of its own stupidity. Rosanna and Sally were never tried.

17

World War II and
Its Effect on Sally

When the tragic attack on Pearl Harbor occurred on December 7, 1941, a lot of lives were changed.

Rationing of food, including sugar, coffee and meat were serious, Gasoline was controlled as well.

San Francisco did not find great changes until the installation of General John L. Dewitt in charge of the Presidio.

The general claimed the disease rate among San Francisco prostitutes was high. While madams were strict disciplinarians when it came to the health and cleanliness of their girls, the District Attorney and the Chief of Police ruled that on May 23rd, all houses must close.

Sex was one of the things the General couldn't ration, so he decided to stop it altogether.

Only a few houses remained open, at least temporarily. Among them were Alice on Bay Street, Mabel Malott at 1275 Bay, Ethel Edwards on Chestnut, Mona Regan on Green Street, and Sally Stanford on Bush.

Everything went along well until a girl named Clara coveted what she thought was a going business at 929 Bush. For years, Clara had a boyfriend who was a lieutenant on the police force.

One night, the lieutenant came to my door and ordered me to close. He told me to lock up and stay locked until he was off that beat. Every time a client would show up, we would see a cop standing in front of the door. The client was naturally scared away.

Clara stopped by one day, and assured Sally that she could take over where I got cut off. Believing that half a loaf was better than none, I made a deal.

Sally later decided to visit the place to see how things were going for Clara. She spotted Clara's cop boyfriend standing outside her door. Sally listened to the conversation from the shadows.

Sure enough, front officials closed Clara's doors. Sally was happy to see her go.

18

Cutting Her Losses

Sally wisely kept other units available if she were forced to close one. This happened when she was forced to close her Bush Street residence.

She owned an apartment building which she was in the process of remodeling.

When finished, the redecorated apartment was indeed beautiful. Wood burning fireplaces with French mantels, wall-to-wall carpets and expensive draperies were all in place.

"Of course," Sally explained, "All the French beds were equipped with Beauty Rest mattresses and Wamsutta sheets. All my male clientele always slept on the best, including genuine down pillows."

Sally made her good friend Rosanna manager of the apartment house. "As long as she was sober," Sally said, "she was great."

One Friday afternoon, Sally picked up her son at the military academy he attended, and they decided to go see Rosanna at the apartment house.

As Sally and her son pulled up at the apartment, Rosanna was talking to a bedraggled woman, with a six-year-old hanging to her dress. She was crying and pleading with Rosanna about something.

The woman's name was Champion. She told me, between tears that she and her son were homeless. She begged me to rent an apartment to her.

I told her she could move into Rosanna's apartment and Rosanna could move into mine. I also gave her a job at $50 a month to clean the apartment. Sally said she turned out to be the cleaningest woman she had ever hired.

Then Sally learned that Mrs. Champion was negotiating with the O.P.A., an office created by the government to regulate rents on scarce apartments. Charging more could bring a regulator down on your neck.

At that time Sally didn't yet own the apartment building but had agreed with the owner that she would buy it if he ever decided to sell. Sally had an appointment with David Blain, the owner, to discuss the apartment house.

As she was getting ready to meet him, her phone rang. On the line was an old friend that said to Sally. "You have an appointment at 929 Bush Street," he said.

He added, "For God's sake, don't talk in that building. The police and the O.P.A. are putting little tin bugs all over the place. If you're at that place right now you probably should hide for a while and you might catch them in the act."

Sally recalled, "Catch them I did." Sally went to the apartment of a tenant next door to her and watched through the peephole in the back door.

She watched as Pete Keneally of the San Francisco Police Department let himself into Sally's apartment with a passkey. As Sally confronted him, he mumbled something about checking the fire escapes. She wondered why a policeman would be checking fire escapes for the fire department.

Since all the bugging equipment was already in the apartment building, Sally decided to call the major newspapers in San Francisco and give them evidence of the bugging activities.

The newspapers and radiomen and photographers came in droves to investigate the evidence.

I stood outside on Bush street and watched the police taking their little tin suitcases out of the apartment house. William T. Wheel, with the O.P.A. walked up to Sally, crumpling an empty pack of Lucky Strikes.

He apologized for what was going on and said that he was only doing his duty. "I said to him, "You've heard about digging a hole too deep."

"Are you threatening me," he asked. I said, "Hell, no. I'm promising you that I'm going to shove you in the hole you dug for me."

He said he was only doing his duty.

The press had a field day with the story. The regional director of the O.P.A. was George Monchard. He blamed Wheel for the fiasco. Wheel blamed the policeman that bugged the building. And the policeman that bugged the building blamed the police chief.

19

The Pacific Ocean Beach Murder

A woman named Jessie Scott Hughes was murdered near her home at a Pacific Ocean beach. A good attempt was made to make it look like the murder was a hit and run accident.

Homicide Chief George Engler had little trouble proving the murder had been committed elsewhere and then laid out at the cul-de-sac street.

Engler found a lot of answers to his mystery. For one thing, he noted that two recently released San Quentin prisoners were in the area.

The homicide detective was determined that Mrs. Hughes was grabbed in her own garage.

She was slugged with a tire iron and then run over with her own car.

No sooner had the two thugs spilled Mrs. Hughes on her own curbstone than they took off for the Latin Quarter. There they stuffed themselves with an expensive Italian dinner.

Mrs. Hughes had just taken out a fifty-thousand-dollar life insurance policy. The beneficiary on the policy was none other than Frank Egan, a public defender.

The whole thing was taking on the air of a dime store detective novel.

Sally Stanford knew that Mrs. Hughes was no shrinking violet. She was truly a she-wolf in friend's clothing. While Mrs. Hughes knew that Frank Egan was a happily married man with young children, she persisted in hounding him.

Sally knew that Egan was a good friend of the doctor that checked the health of Sally's girls. She had a hunch that more was in the picture than could be seen.

Sally called the health doctor. "I asked him if he and Egan had discussed the San Quentin prisoners in his office within the past couple of days? He said he had."

Not only that, but the two prisoners were former clients of Public Defender Egan, as was the victim, Mrs. Hughes.

Sally urged the doctor to search his office thoroughly, including the light fixture for a bug. In a moment, the doctor told her he had found the device.

Confirmation of this came later when Chief of Police Charles Dullea told the press he had put a tap on the doctor's phone.

Egan sent his wife Lorraine to retain Attorney Vincent Hallinan, the fiery left-wing Irish lawyer who was just beginning to burn up the California courts.

During Egan's trial, ruthless Judge Frank Dunn found Hallinan in contempt of court and ordered him to jail.

The two ex-cons accused of killing Mrs. Hughes claimed that Egan had hired them to kill Mrs. Hughes. Based on this testimony, Egan was convicted.

20

San Francisco's Vigilance Committee

During the Gold Rush period, in the year 1851, a group of 700 men formed the San Francisco Vigilance Committee.

It targeted prostitution. In its initial efforts, the vigilantes confined their efforts to eradicating vice establishments that catered to people of color.

The City's first anti-prostitution laws were passed in 1854. Enforcement of this law was almost exclusively against Mexican, Chilean, and Chinese.

Sophie Breider, a student at Claremont McKenna College, did her senior thesis on "The Best Bad Things": An Analytical History of Madams of Gold Rush San Francisco."

We thought her study was important enough to be printed in part in this book.

In her dissertation, Brieder quotes Hinton Harper Helper, who wrote in 1849, "It is my unbiased opinion that California can and does furnish the best bad things obtainable in America."

One of those "bad things," Helper says, "was prostitution."

The Gold Rush era in San Francisco was roughly the years 1848 to 1856. This era permitted some of the most famous and most socially acceptable opportunities for vice in American history.

The American imagination has created an image of a madam. And the fictional representations of them does not stray far from the image of "beautiful, young, white, witty and perfect," Brieder wrote.

In 1848, when gold drove men West, most women stayed behind. San Francisco was home to only 200 women. "Sex work became not only viable, but a profitable and acceptable occupation for women."

As gold brought hundreds of thousands to California, it also expanded the market for prostitution. In just two years, more than 2,000 women arrived in San Francisco. Their arrival was certainly welcomed by the male population.

Belle Cora and Ah Toy were the most famous of the early San Francisco Gold Rush madams. They inspired many characteristics of the American madam.

"While women empowered themselves during the California Gold Rush through prostitution, they were as quickly stripped of their power with the arrival of institutions of power to California.

Once the railroad, telegraph and American Government reached San Francisco, white patriarchy was able to establish control. Not all vice vanished during this Americanization period.

While prostitution was hard hit, liquor use wasn't. Still, the legacy of the madam has endured throughout American history.

21

Belle Cora

Her name was Arabella Ryan. She was the daughter of an illustrious Baltimore minister and arrived in San Francisco in 1849. Traveling with her was her Italian Catholic lover, Charles Cora.

Belle was only 22 and was said to be a voluptuous character. She arrived in San Francisco aboard the steamer Falcon, from New Orleans. Charles Cora was a well-known gambler there and Belle was a lesser-known prostitute.

The Coras found great success in San Francisco, garnering an impressive fortune from gambling and prostitution. Cora, financed by Charles, quickly became San Francisco's most successful madam.

Cora flaunted beauty and wealth on the gayest thoroughfares, and on every gay occasion, with senator, judge, and citizen at her beck and call.

H.H. Bancroft characterizes Cora as San Francisco's first madam.

She opened a house on Dupont Street. In doing so, Belle became one of San Francisco's greatest celebrities. The parlor house's luxury and glamor rivaled those of the New Orleans brothels.

Cora's parlor house on Dupont Street burned down less than a year after it opened. Cora rebuilt quickly in Waverly Place, near Pike Street, in the same luxurious fashion.

She attracted a high-class clientele. The regular parties and balls hosted by Cora reflected the overall social acceptance of prostitution during this era in San Francisco.

Following the simple rule of supply and demand, Cora was able to charge handsomely for the services of her beautiful girls. Consequently, Belle and Charles became one of the richest couples in San Francisco.

Payments in her sex parlor were made in gold ore, each payment was weighed on a scale in the parlor house.

Until 1839, women legally were bound to their husbands with no access to their own property or earnings under the common legal system.

This system required women to surrender their rights to their husbands upon marriage.

This system allowed people like Belle Cora to remain unmarried, become wealthy and powerful economic actors on their own right. Belle's choice to remain unmarried was her greatest act of political independence.

Even after the passage of the first vice laws, which criminalized prostitution in 1854, Cora was able to continue running her parlor house. She could remain undisturbed because of her connections to Frank Soule, John G. Gihon, and James Nisbet.

Because of her connections during the prime Gold Rush years, Belle Cora was not only financially well off, but powerful politically.

It wasn't until the gold ran out and the Gold Rush ended that attention was turned to curbing vice.

While Belle and Charles were seated in the first balcony of San Francisco's newest theater, the attention Belle was receiving infuriated and embarrassed Mrs. William Richardson, seated directly in from of Belle. Mrs. Richardson's husband was a U.S. Marshall.

Her husband demanded that the Coras leave the theater. Belle and Charles considered their standing as above a U.S. Marshall and refused to leave. The Coras continued to enjoy the play, while the Richardsons left.

In a later confrontation between Charles Cora and Marshall Richardson, Cora was accused of shooting the Marshall. Charles Cora was arrested.

Belle hired a reputable lawyer. Charles' trial ended up in a hung jury. A second trial found him guilty. He was sentenced to death.

In her attempts to exonerate Charles, Belle spent a good portion of her wealth. Publicity and scandal forced her to close her parlor house.

On the morning of his execution, Belle married Charles in order to inherit his estate.

22

Ah Toy

On February 2,1848, the steamship, *The Eagle,* brought the first Chinese woman to San Francisco. She was employed as a domestic with a merchant family. Her name has seemingly been lost to history.

Later, in the same year, two more Chinese women arrived, one of which became well-known in San Francisco. This was the 20-year old Ah Toy. As one of only three Chinese women in California, Ah Toy made herself known to the men of the Gold Rush.

Soon after arrival, Ah Toy rented a room in an alley off Clay Street, which soon grew into a flourishing China Town. Ah Toy worked as an independent prostitute from her home on Clay Street.

Despite growing anti-Chinese sentiment in the City, the men took a quick liking to Ah Toy.

Within three months, Ah Toy's house could easily be recognized. There was always a line of men waiting for a turn with the fascinating Ah Toy.

Her rise to fame, or infamy, depending on the perspective, seemed unprecedented. Ah Toy was clever enough to capitalize on her newly found acclaim.

When news spread of Ah Toy's success as a young unmarried woman, her independent powerful status was challenged. A man in Hong Kong wrote to leaders of the Chinese community in San Francisco that he was Ah Toy's husband.

Ah Toy chose to defend herself in a San Francisco Court. She denied the claims and asked the judge to allow her to remain in San Francisco to better her life.

She won her case.

After her first appearance in a San Francisco court in 1849, Ah Toy became increasingly comfortable with using the courts against her customers.

Newspaper reporters became fascinated with Ah Toys manner of dress. Her apricot-colored satin jacket and willow green pantaloons became the subject of news stories, as did the colorful tabis on her small tightly bound feet.

Ah Toy registered a complaint in Judge George Baker's Court that several of her clients were cheating her of gold which she weighed herself.

They were paying for her services with brass filings rather than gold.

By filing criminal charges in Judge Baker's courtroom, Ah Toy effectively revealed her profession.

Although Judge Baker denied Ah Toy's complaint. Ah Toy became a celebrity in San Francisco. Newspapers noted her charisma and boldness in coming forward.

When asked to name names of customers who had defrauded her, Ah Toy not only named names but pointed to several men in the courtroom.

In 1850, five more Chinese women arrived in San Francisco. Two of them sought employment with Ah Toy. This meant that Toy successfully transitioned herself as a madam.

Ah Toy's glory days did not last long. The year 1851 was the beginning of her decline. The formation of the San Francisco Vigilance Committee was formed by a group of men to bring law and order to the city.

The committee gathered initially to address the influx violent immigrants. The committee focused on the Australia ex-convicts, notably the Sydney Ducks. Four of the Sydney Ducks were hung by the committee.

The Vigilance next turned its efforts toward prostitution. While prostitution was legal in San Francisco in 1851, it was also extremely popular. The vigilance committee turned a deaf ear to the popularity.

It appointed a special patrol, headed by John A. Clark, to investigate the city's prostitution and brothels.

Clark was charmed with Ah Toy. Rather than investigating her, Clark became her lover. This provided several years of relief for Ah Toy from the Vigilance committee and allowed Ah Toy to expand her business.

Despite the benefit from her relationship with Clark, anti-Chinese sentiment was growing. Ah Toy could not insulate herself from it.

In 1852, a new wave of Chinese migration hit San Francisco. Many San Franciscans held Ah Toy responsible.

Several hundred Chinese girls and women arrived in the city. Ah Toy's brothel expanded. She now had 40 women in her employ.

During her last trial of 1852, Ah Toy enjoyed her last victory in the San Francisco legal system. In this case, she had filed charges against a Chinese boss for trying to impose illegal taxes on Chinese women. She won the case.

In 1854, the City passed Ordinance 546, "To Suppress Houses of Ill Fame Within City Limits". Ah Toy did not immediately close her brothel. She was fined $20 for keeping a disorderly house.

The Foreign Miners Tax of 1850 was brought into play. When it was declared unconstitutional, the Foreign Miners License Tax of 1852 was employed.

The Supreme Court disallowed Chinese individuals from testifying against white people.

Ah Toy was arrested and convicted in 1854. She was arrested several more times over the next three years as she continued to conduct business as a madam in San Francisco.

She announced she was closing her business in 1857. She told reporters she was leaving and had no intentions of returning. She sold her house and apparently left the city.

She returned in 1859 and reopened her house. She was again arrested for "house keeping".

After that arrest, Ah Toy apparently had enough. She left San Francisco and never returned.

Word spread that Ah Toy had simply moved south 40 miles to San Jose where she reportedly married a wealthy Chinese man.

After he died, Ah Toy was said to have started selling clams and continued until her death. She died within days of her 100th birthday.

23

Mary Ann Conklin

Most of what is known about Mary Ann Conklin is hearsay and legend, which increases her interest as a character. She is said to have married a whaling captain named David "Bull" Conklin in 1851.

In 1853 he abandoned her in Port Townsend, Washington, and headed for Alaska.

Mary Ann became the manager of the Felker House, a hotel and brothel. She gained a reputation for running a clean place with good food.

She had an equally well-known reputation for swearing like the proverbial sailor. She developed her cursing ability while at sea and could swear in English, French, Spanish, German, Portuguese and Chinese,

Her fluency in swearing earned her the nickname, "Mother Damnable".

Her flamboyant personality and larger-than-life character resulted in the hotel becoming known as The Conklin House. There are epic stories about how she ran her business.

When the City of Seattle government decided to hold a lynching trial in the hotel, they asked for a receipt. Mary Ann was so outraged that she started throwing firewood at people when her yelling didn't suffice.

She was always surrounded by dogs that were about as hostile as she was.

Mary Ann Conklin died in 1873, but that didn't end her story. In 1884, graves in Seattle Cemetery were moved in preparation for turning the area into a park.

Legend says when they dug up Madame Damnable, her coffin was so heavy it had to be opened to see what was inside.

Supposedly, Mary Ann had turned to stone, thwarting even the worms that would have otherwise eaten her.

24

Painted Ladies
Of the Wild West

Victorian prudence taught women that the sexual act was strictly for the bearing of children. Men of the West were often intimidated by the "decent" woman who laid down the moral law.

Sometimes these men simply found it more comfortable with the "Painted Ladies" that had no such rules as moral laws.

Most every Old West town had at least a couple of "shady ladies" somewhere in the neighborhood. Sometimes they might be disguised as a person who does laundry, as a seamstress or some who runs a boarding house.

Madam Pearl De Vere

One such person was Pearl de Vere, of Cripple Creek, Colorado. She arrived in Cripple Creek during the silver panic of 1893.

Pearl de Vere was known in Denver as Mrs. Martin. She had amassed a small fortune for her services to wealthy gentlemen in town. Pearl de Vere proved wise when she moved to Cripple Creek.

She bought a small frame house on Myers Avenue and opened it up for business. It was an overnight success.

Pearl, at 31 years-old, was described as a red-haired, strong-willed business woman. Pearl had the most beautiful ladies of any in the area. They wore fine clothing, received monthly medical checks and were well-paid.

The madam didn't hesitate to show her ladies off to the community. She drove her girls about town in an open carriage, pulled by a team of fine black horses.

Pearl was dressed in a different outfit on each outing. Her clothes were the envy of every neighborhood woman, and the men stared at her with longing.

The women of Cripple Creek were horrified that Pearl and her girls dared to shop on Bennett Avenue where the fashionable women of Cripple Creek liked to shop.

Marshall Wilson finally regulated the shopping hours of the "girls", allowing them to visit the store only during off-hours. In addition, each working girl paid a $6 monthly tax, and madams had to pay $16.

Children were forbidden to walk near Myers Avenue and were told to shield their eyes when Madam Pearl paraded by in her carriage.

111

Pearl soon met a man named C.B. Flynn, the owner of a sawmill. They married in 1895, but Pearl still ran her profitable business. Soon after they were married a fire raged through the camp.

The fire destroyed most of the business district in town as well as Pearl's bawdy house. The fire also ruined Flynn financially.

He accepted a job in Monterrey. Mexico. Pearl remained in Cripple Creek, intent on rebuilding her business.

She built the finest parlor house the city had ever seen. It was a two-story brick building that she called "The Old Homestead". She imported wallpaper from Paris, outfitted the house with the finest hardwood furniture and high-grade carpets.

The house included a telephone and an intercom system, and two bathrooms, unheard of during that time.

Her four beautiful women made Pearl's house the most whispered about place in town. At $250 a night, only the extremely wealthy could afford to visit. At the time, $3 a day was considered a good wage.

Pearl held lavish parties at The Old Homestead. She brought in tropical flowers and served food and drink.

She was called upon to throw a high-brow party by a wealthy admirer from Poverty Gulch. Towns people watch as cases of champagne, Russian caviar and Alabama Wild Turkey were carted into the parlor.

Arriving next were two orchestras from Denver. Pearl was resplendent in an $800 shell pink chiffon gown, complete with sequins and seed pearls.

Pearl had too much to drink and excused herself, going to her bedroom. When one of her girls checked on her, she was lying in bed still draped in the chiffon gown. She was breathing heavily.

When the girl couldn't wake her, a doctor was called. It was too late. Pearl De Vere died at the age of thirty-six. The coroner attributed her death to an accidental overdose of morphine to induce sleep.

Her sister in Indiana was notified and made the long train trip west. She had always thought Pearl was a dressmaker. When she learned of Pearl's true profession, she refused to have anything to do with her sister's remains.

It was found later that Pearl's estate didn't have enough money to bury her properly. Pearls friends suggested auctioning off her pink gown. Before that could be done, however, a $1,000 check arrived from Denver with written instructions directing that Pearl be buried in her pink gown.

Pearl was interred with much pomp and circumstance, the funeral parade being led by the Elks Band and escorted by four mounted policemen.

Pearl's pink and lavender casket covered with red and white roses, was lowered into her grave at the foot of Mt. Pisgah Cemetery. The grave was marked with a wooden marker.

In 1930, Cripple Creek was holding Cripple Creek Days. Someone suggested a story on Pearl De Vere.

Her grave had become lost in a weed-filled corner of the cemetery and her name had eroded away from the marker.

25

Madam Lou Bunch
Was a Heavyweight

Madam Lou Bunch weighed 300 pounds.

Louisa "Lou" Bunch ran the most successful brothel in Central City, Colorado. Gold was pouring from Colorado mines during the late 1800s, and Madam Bunch was just trying to grab her share of it.

Her house was located on Pine Street near the gold miners who were working their claims.

When a tuberculosis epidemic struck the area, threatening to wipe out Central City's population, Madam Lou put her girls to work. Lou converted her sporting house into a makeshift hospital.

Lou knew that the town's economy and her business depended on healthy miners.

The town has never forgotten Lou Bunch's efforts. "Lou Bunch Day" is celebrated every second weekend of June. One of the day's most popular events is the Madam Lou Bunch Bed Race.

In the bed races, a man and a woman sit in a brass bed while a second man pushes them down the street. The bed races take place down Main Street and teams of three (two men and one woman) race the over-sized brass beds on wheels.

There are prizes for 1st, 2nd, and 3rd, along with a prize for the best costume. There is live music, a parade and the Madam and Miner's Ball.

The streets become lined with hundreds of people for the Lou Bunch Day activities.

Perhaps the weirdest celebration is the "Headless Chicken Day". This began when a chicken named Mike survived the chopping block with his brain stem still intact.

With the help of water and grain, delivered through an eyedropper, Mike survived for 18 months.

On the first weekend in June, in *Fruita, Colorado*, there is a disc golf tournament, a rooster-calling contest and a poultry show.

Then, there's the fruit-cake toss in Manitou Springs. Here contestants toss a fruit cake to determine accuracy and speed. There's also a fruit-cake costume competition.

If these contests don't whet your appetite, you might consider the *Frozen Dead Guy Day* in Nederland, Colorado. Here, homage is paid to a man whose body has been cryogenically preserved on dry ice for the past 30 years.

This story involves

Bredo Morstoel, of Norway, whose grandson Trygve Bauge, had him cryogenically preserved. The grandson had hoped to build his own cryogenics lab. His plans ended when he was deported.

26

Lola Montez

Lola Montez

Lola Montez became famous despite her lack of talent. She was born in Ireland with her birth name being Marie Dolores Eliza Rosanna Gilbert.

Her mother, Elizabeth Oliver was the daughter of a former High Sheriff of Cork, and a member of Parliament for Kilmallock in County Limerick.

There are multiple discrepancies concerning the birth of Eliza Gilbert, who later became Lola Montez. She was a stubborn and belligerent child.

At age 19, she eloped with Lieutenant Thomas James. They separated five years later.

Cut off financially by her mother Eliza Gilbert, Lola launched her career as a dancer. She cast off the name, Eliza Gilbert, and became Lola Montez. She also developed a fictional biography.

Lola opened her show in London as "Lola Montez, the Spanish Dancer'.

During her travels she is said to have formed relationships with such notables as Franz Liszt and Alexandre Dumas.

Listz was born in 1811. He was a Hungarian pianist and rather a bounder. He had an affair and children with Marie diAgoult. He later lived with Princess Carolyne zu Sayn-Wittgenstein. He wrote more than 700 piano compositions.

While dancing in Munich, Louis I of Bavaria was so struck by her beauty that he offered her a castle. She accepted and became the Baroness and Countess of Landsfeld.

She literally took over the cabinet of her Husband. It became known at point as "*Lolaministerium*". Louis' infatuation with Lola helped bring down his regime in the Revolution of 1848.

In March 1848, Louis abdicated, and Lola fled to London. She married the wealthy Lt. George Heald in 1849, although she had never been divorced from her husband Thomas James. Heald left her.

Lola then took her tour to the United States. She modified her act to include her notorious "*Spider Dance*" that concluded many of her performances. She engaged in her third marriage, this time to Patrick P. Hull, of San Francisco. This marriage, too, ended in divorce.

She moved to Grass Valley, California. Among her diversions there was the coaching of a young girl named Lotta Crabtree in singing and dancing.

Montez then settled in New York City after an unsuccessful tour of Australia.

Lola took her act west where she met and married newspaper editor Patrick Purdy Hall. Predictably, the marriage lasted only a few months.

As Lola's extravagant living exhausted her funds, she took to the lecture stage. Her talks drew large audiences.

Her health became poor and she had to give up the lecture circuit. Having spent most of her lecture funds, she spent her last days in New York City, where she died on January 17, 1861, at the age of 42.

27

Mattie Silks

Mattie Silks

Mattie Silks made one thing clear. She did not work as a prostitute.

She was Colorado's most successful madam, and proud of it.

She was a businesswoman first and the madam of a posh whorehouse second, but she did not turn tricks herself.

Mattie said she had a firm rule. "I never took a girl into my house who had had no previous experience of life and men. That was a rule of mine."

No innocent young girl was ever hired by me. And they came to me for the same reasons that I hired them. Because there was money in it for all of us.

Mattie opened her house in Denver to attract the silver and gold prospectors raging in the state at the time.

Her house was a three-story brick mansion with 27 rooms, including 16 bedrooms, 4 parlors, and a ballroom with a 16-foot round mirror set in the ceiling.

A trip upstairs with one of Mattie's girls cost anywhere from ten dollars to two-hundred-dollars. On a ten-dollar trick, Mattie kept four-dollars.

Mattie insisted that all her men customers be treated as gentlemen. The girls were allowed to sit only on the ottomans scattered around the parlor area, not on the chairs and never on the laps of the male guests.

The rule was, "Be a lady in the drawing room and a whore in the bedroom." Once the doors were closed it was "anything goes."

One madam that practiced her trade in both Texas and Oklahoma, described the business, "I've laid it in all of 'em. I throwed my fanny twenty-one times a night, five bucks a throw.

By the time old red-eye came up, I was eatin' breakfast drunker'n an Indian."

Mattie is thought to have been born in Terre Haute or Gary, Indiana, 1846 to 1848, and to have run away from home at age thirteen. Her given name is not recorded, but on certain documents pertaining to her, including her death certificate, the first name Martha was used.

According to Clark Secrest, in his *Hell's Belles, Prostitution, Vice, and Crime in Early Denver,* an envelope found under the flooring of one of her Market Street houses was addressed to "Miss Maté Weinman. She is not known to have ever used that name.

Her death certificate asserted that her father and mother were unknown.

At age nineteen, in Springfield, Illinois, Mattie opened her first "sporting house". She maintained she had never been a prostitute herself and bragged that she was unique in this respect.

She told Janie Green, another Denver madam, that she had recruited three girls from Abilene, Kansas, and one from Dodge City, and headed west. Her new employees worked from a tent along the way.

With the tent as a traveling bordello, Mattie and her four girls headed for the Colorado mountains, carrying along the first portable bathtub to enter the mining camps. Their initial stop was Jamestown, northwest of Boulder.

From there, Mattie proceeded to Georgetown.

It was apparently when she ran her Springfield brothel back in Illinois in 1864 that she coined the name of "Silks" for a last name.

She adopted it because of her love for silk materials. Little or nothing is known of her childhood. She died without revealing any of the secrets of her early years, including her true name.

The gold and silver mines of Colorado were literally pouring rich ore out of its veins and *The Bawdy House Girls* were raking it in as fast as the miners could dig it out of the ground.

In Denver, the cribs operated by the prostitutes were little different from the red-light districts of other gold rush towns. These cribs were lined up shoulder-to-shoulder and were barely wide enough for a door and a front window.

The standard rental for such a place was twenty-five dollars a week, paid in advance. It is here that the street-walkers and the one-dollar whores hung out. The going rate was one-dollar if the girl was white and four-bits if she was black.

Madams operating the parlor houses forbid their girls from associating with the crib girls. This was to justify their higher prices. The parlor house madams wanted their clientele to understand that their merchandise was higher quality.

In Georgetown, Colorado, Mattie Silks operated one of the five parlor houses on Brownell Street. The area was often described as "the richest square mile on earth." It was likewise the source of Mattie Silks' great wealth.

It was also in Georgetown that Mattie met the love of her life, a handsome Texan by the name of Cortese D. Thomson. While he was handsome, lithe and lean, Thomson was also a sponger of the worst type.

Thomson was a professional "foot racer", a sporting event that once attracted gamblers by the droves. The sport was fading fast at the time that Mattie met her man.

Mattie's consort, the handsome Cort Thomson, (middle row, seated, without striped stockings, organized foot-racing contests between volunteer fire departments.

Even though Thomson spent Mattie's money as fast he could convince her to give it to him, she still worshiped him.

While Mattie was not bad looking, she was rather short and always appeared "over-weight".

The handsome "Cort" was not only tall, but a few years younger than Mattie. She considered him a real prize.

Some estimates figure Mattie doled out as much as seventy-five-thousand dollars to Cort, which he lost gambling and playing the big spender. He also cheated on Mattie.

In 1876, Mattie moved from Georgetown to Denver. Cort, naturally, accompanied her as she was his own personal money source.

Her first property in Denver was 501 McGaa Street, which she occupied for years.

She brought in twelve young and good looking "boarders" to occupy the many rooms in the house.

Mattie's parlor house of twelve *bawdy* girls did so well she invested in another. This one she rented out to Jennie Rogers, a dashing brunette that had the elegance that Mattie desired but never could achieve.

While Mattie loved expensive silks, her taste in clothes was pitiful, even though costly. Her costumes appeared Victorian and almost comical rather than stylish.

When Mattie and Cort returned from a trip to Europe, they found Denver and its red-light district virtually deserted. The gold rush had moved to Alaska and the Yukon. A rich gold strike had been made in the Klondike.

Mattie and Cort moved with the strike, taking along her bevy of twelve boarders.

Mattie rented a house for four-hundred dollars a month in Dawson and paid fifty dollars a day in protection to the Dawson police.

She had never made so much money so quickly as she did in Dawson. Still, the weather was atrocious, and she feared Cort was catching pneumonia. She decided to pull up stakes and returned to Denver. She reopened her Denver parlor.

Because Cort was drinking too much, Mattie wanted to get him away from town and the temptations of alcohol.

With financing from Mattie, Cort bought three pieces of land in the little town of Wray, east of Denver.

It wasn't long before his neighbors were accusing him of running off their stock and altering the brands. When Mattie visited Cort, she immediately disliked the way Cort was operating.

She discharged Cort's foreman, a man known locally as Dirty Face Murphy, and hired in his place Jack Ready, a tall and handsome mountain of a man.

Cort soon became ill. A doctor diagnosed the cause as a severe attack of stomach cramps, believed to be caused by cirrhosis of the liver and excessive drinking. He gave Mattie a bottle of laudanum, and suggested she lace Cort's whiskey with it as needed.

She followed the doctor's orders throughout the night, but at daybreak, Cort was pronounced dead.

Mattie, herself, soon married her new foreman, Jack Ready. He acted as her bookkeeper and bouncer for the drunks who frequently staggered into the house during the night.

Ready remained with Mattie through the years. She died in 1929 at the age of eighty-three.

28

Julia Bulette

Julia Bullette emigrated from London to New Orleans as a very young girl. She was said to have married at one time to a man named Smith. No one knows if that was his true name or not.

She separated from her husband and traveled to California about 1852, She lived in Weaverville, a small town in Trinity County before moving to Virginia City, Nevada.

She was a prostitute in the bustling gold camp of Virginia City, but she was a respected one.

For Virginia City Engine Company No. 1, Virginia City's volunteer fire department, "Jule" Bulette was special. She worked the brakes when the firemen went on calls. She was an honorary member of the firemen's brigade.

Virginia City was born by the discovery of the Comstock Mine. Saloons sprouted faster than did miner's tents. And as soon as there was a saloon or a boarding house opened, it had prostitutes and dance-hall girls ready to give pleasure to the miners, all for a price that is.

Makeshift "cribs" quickly sprang up along "D" Street in Virginia City. There were high-class prostitutes, simple streetwalkers and women that had succumbed to alcohol or drug addiction all trying to get their pinch of gold dust from the miners' poke.

One section of "C" street was called "The Barbary Coast," adapted from the famous Barbary Coast in San Francisco. In a short time, the Barbary Coast in Virginia City was said to be twice as evil as the one in San Francisco, which was certainly no slouch in that category.

In 1863, Virginia City's Board of Aldermen passed an ordinance against houses of prostitution. It was an effort to cut down the lawlessness and debauchery attached to them.

The Virginia Evening Bulletin reported:

The Board of Aldermen, at their meeting on the 13th, took action upon the many nuisances at present existing in our midst in the shape of houses of ill fame, and passed a stringent ordinance against their existence in so central a part of town.

We are glad to see the Board have some regard for the morality of the city, and their recent action has met the hearty approval of our citizens.

The first section of the ordinance says that it shall be unlawful to open or maintain any house of ill-repute or brothel in the district of this city west of D street, or south of Sutton Avenue or north of Mill street; and the second section sets forth that any owner of a house or property included in the district in this city who shall let, hire or rent his or her property for the occupancy of women of bad or immoral character, shall give and pay to the city five hundred dollars. Some may consider this rather stringent, but we do not, and we hope to see the provisions of the ordinance carried into effect.

The ordinance had hardly been passed when a fire swept through the area, destroying a number of buildings occupied by prostitutes. The ladies simply moved to other quarters outside the restricted area.

In 1874, The Virginia and Truckee Railroad Company purchased the burned-out property to continue their railroad and to build a depot. The company graded the property to locate warehouses, depot premises and sidetracks.

The prostitutes still in the area were warned to vacate their houses or be plowed under, but many stayed, rent free, until the last moment.

They then found new buildings to occupy and carry on their trade.

The citizens continued to complain about the lewd women and shameless men occupying the dens of inequity in their midst but other than an occasional arrest, little was done to move the ladies of the evening out of town.

Julia Bulette's background is a bit obscured among its historical fallacies.

It is believed she was born in London but immigrated to New Orleans at a very young age. Details are sparse, but some historians claim she was married there to a man named "Smith".

Whether real or fictional, she was separated from him and traveled to California in 1852. Settling first in the town of Weaverville, she worked as a prostitute before moving to Virginia City in 1863.

Some writers trifle even more with her background, claiming she was a mulatto born in Natchez, Mississippi and worked as a prostitute in New Orleans. Guy Rocha, Nevada State archivist dispels that as complete fiction.

Rocha says contrary to some writers, Julia wore silk, velvet and sable furs. Neither was she making one thousand dollars a night for her services, for which she accepted gold bars of bullion, diamonds or rubies.

"She was neither wealthy, beautiful, willowy, nor did the rather heavy-set woman seemingly float when she walked," Rocha says, declaring much of what was written about her was myth.

What is true is that Julia met a horrible death at thirty-seven years of age.

She was strangled and clubbed with the handle of a pistol while lying in bed.

About 11:30 p.m. Saturday, January 18, Julia said goodnight to her next-door neighbor, Gertrude Holmes (also a prostitute), telling her she had to meet a miner that was coming to see her.

At 11 a.m., Sunday, a Chinese houseboy came in and built a fire but was careful not to disturb her, thinking she was asleep. At 11:30, her body was discovered by her friend Gertrude, who came to call her to breakfast.

The bed covers on either side of the body were not disturbed, so it was obvious she had not shared the bed with anyone. A coroner's report said she had been struck with the handle of a pistol and beaten with an eighteen-inch stick of firewood.

Clear imprints of fingers and a thumb remained on her throat. Many of her finer pieces of jewelry and clothing were missing.

Julia was buried on Monday, the day following her death. Her funeral procession included the Metropolitan Brass Band, about sixty members of the volunteer fire department marching on foot, and sixteen carriages of mourners. Included were her friends among the sisterhood of prostitutes.

Helping to solve Julia's murder was the fact that the villain didn't leave town. Martha Camp, a friend of Julia's, was awakened by someone approaching her door. When she screamed, her attacker fled.

Martha, however, had gotten a clear view of the man. A short time later, she recognized him on the street and reported it to the police.

The man's name was Jean Marie A. Villain, a Frenchman that worked in a bakery on D street. Villain had adopted the name of John Millian. He spoke very little English.

A break in Julia Bulette's murder came from a Mrs. Cazentre, of Gold Hill, just outside of Virginia City. She told police she had purchased a dress that once belonged to Julia Bulette from John Millian for forty dollars. Millian told her he was selling the dress for a widow whose husband had been killed in the Ophir mine.

The dress was positively identified as belonging to Julia by dry goods merchant Sam Rosener, who said he sold the dress to Julia himself. He had acquired the entire shipment of that particular pattern when it arrived in San Francisco.

The accused Millian had also left a trunk in storage at the bakery where he worked. When the trunk was searched, nearly all of Julia's missing clothing and other items were inside.

A jury convicted Millian to hang. At 12:42 p.m., April 24, 1868, the killer was brought before three-thousand onlookers and marched up the gallows steps.

Julia's death brought her more notoriety than did her activities as a prostitute.

29

The Girls of Santa Cruz

S anta Cruz County, California officials took a dim view of prostitution early on. The first known arrest for keeping a house of ill-fame took place in Watsonville, in 1860.

Nuanor Samilla and Filleppe Escalante were jailed. Each were charged with a misdemeanor, found guilty, and given a fine of fifteen-dollars.

The next attempt at curbing the ill-famed houses in Santa Cruz came in 1868. Two men, by the names of Malson and Shaw, were tried on a charge of keeping a house. They were released when the jury failed to agree on a verdict.

Like many western towns, the only effort to curb prostitution came from the annual grand jury meetings.

In Santa Cruz County, it became a time-honored ritual for the grand jury to probe the towns houses of ill-repute after they had looked at the conditions at the poor farm or the jail.

Writer Phil Read, in an article titled "Harlots and Whorehouses," noted that the grand juries of 1872 and 1877 showed more determination than usual in shutting down the brothels.

They adopted the motto "Let the Augean Stables be cleansed," showing a flair for classical literature in its reference to Hercules cleaning thirty years of refuse from the stables of Augeas in one day.

In 1872, the Santa Cruz County grand jury indicted sixteen people, including the three most famous Santa Cruz madams. These were Emma Cooper, Maria McDermott and Madame Pauline.

Not all prostitutes were degraded and down-trodden. Madame Pauline was a good example. She was a familiar figure on the streets of Santa Cruz for thirty years.

She owned three brothels in the county and was known to do good deeds throughout those years.

Even the normally chaste *Santa Cruz Sentinel* eulogized Madame Pauline in this way: "In a quiet way, she did many charitable acts. No poor person ever came away from her empty handed. More than one poor family she assisted, and the world was none the wiser."

When the 1877 grand jury attempted to close down all of the houses of prostitution, a group of prominent citizens, including a number of women, decided to take action.

They sent a petition to the District Attorney, asking him to defer prosecuting Madame Pauline. Their petition read, "...she was a liberal and spirited citizen, contributing generously to charitable and public projects...and that she had given something to bring the Santa Cruz Railroad into our town..."

Sheriff Bob Orton still raided the Front Street brothels in 1877. To his chagrin, a newspaper article on May 12, 1877, supported Madame Pauline.

"Pauline, proprietress of a house of prostitution, has kept a very orderly and quiet house. This house was completely unobjectionable to even the nearest neighbors."

Madame Pauline was born Florinni De Paulinni in 1847 in New York City. She was married twice. Her first husband was George Prince and her second was Jim Ogden. Both ended in divorce and left her with three children to support.

She arrived in Watsonville, California in 1867 and began work in a brothel on Pajaro Street. By 1871, Pauline had saved enough money to buy the house where she worked.

She later invested in other real estate in the downtown area of Watsonville.

The following year, she moved her brothel operation to Santa Cruz while retaining her interests in Watsonville.

Her children did well. Ironically, perhaps, her daughter, Edna Ogden, entered a convent at San Bernardino and rose to the position of Mother Superior of her order.

Madame Pauline always remained close to her family, including her oldest son, Pearly Prince, a land agent for the Southern Pacific Railroad in the Los Angeles area, and a second son, who was in real estate in San Francisco.

When underage boys walked timidly into her parlor, Pauline good-naturedly escorted them down the back stairs and out the door.

In 1885, her neighbor Dr. Benjamin Knight approached Pauline. He told her about a patient of his that was about to give birth. He described her house as in a state of complete disarray. The pregnant woman lay on a pile of blankets in the middle of the floor in critical condition.

The only furnishings in the house were two chairs, a rickety bench, and one worn-out table upon which rested three potatoes, the only food the family had.

What touched the doctor even more were the faces of the six children standing silently about the room, all in need of clothes. The eldest girl wore a dress fashioned from an old grain sack.

Dr. Knight had willingly donated his medical services, but he feared for the plight of the children.

The following day, Madame Pauline hired a buggy, rode out to the house of the family, and brought them all back to town.

She moved them into a frame house she owned on Water Street and put the father to work doing maintenance on her various properties.

Madame Pauline died of apoplexy at her home in 1898 at the age of fifty-one. Her estate was valued at more than forty-thousand-dollars.

The Santa Cruz grand jury might have wished it hadn't stirred up the wrath of feisty Jane Allison in 1877. She mounted a formidable challenge to the local system of jurisprudence.

When Lady Jane was done, she left half the male population in town blushing.

When Jane was called before the court on a charge of prostitution and disorderly conduct, she vowed to fight the charge, even "if it took all summer."

To represent her, Jane hired lawyer Joseph Skirm, a determined representative of underdogs. He was also considered perhaps the most brilliant barrister in Santa Cruz County.

When Judge Albert Hagan called the court to order, Jane and her attorney sat quietly as the jury was impaneled and Attorney John Logan presented the people's case.

Attorney Skirm then approached the bench and informed the judge he had a list of witnesses he wanted subpoenaed.

When the judge asked for the list, Jane stood up, took out her little black book, and read a total of one-hundred-forty names, including most of the male residents of Santa Cruz.

Attorney Skirm had a field day with his cross-examination of the witnesses. Most sat intimidated with Jane's presence in the courtroom.

When all the arguments were heard, the jury retired for deliberations. The jury rapped on the jury-room door, saying they had not been able to agree.

The court refused to let them out, keeping them locked up for another two hours. Judge Hagan, Attorney Skirm and Jane Allison all adjourned to a nearby restaurant for a leisurely supper.

Judge Hagan then called the jury back into the court. They were still unable to agree. The judge called a mistrial and sent the panel home.

Jane Allison returned to work at Emma Cooper's whorehouse.

30

Mary Ellen Pleasant

At birth, Mary Ellen Pleasant had no last name. She said she was the illegitimate child of a Virginia governor's son (John H. Pleasants) and an enslaved Haitian Voodoo priestess. (As used in this context, the word "Voodoo" means spirit, and refers to the religion descended from a number of African cultures.)

While she won many of her frequent battles against inequities for others, Mary Ellen was never quite able to win the battle for her own good name.

Mary Ellen was born a slave near Augusta, Georgia between 1814 and 1817. According to ship's records and confirming testimony, Mary Ellen arrived in San Francisco in 1852 to escape persecution under the Fugitive Slave Law of 1850.

As a child, she was sent to work in the service of a merchant in Nantucket, Massachusetts.

She was a precocious child, and according to her final memoir, could recall the entire day's transactions in the general store where she clerked. This was indeed a feat, in that Mary Ellen could barely read and write.

When her indenture ended in 1841, Mary Ellen married James W. Smith, a wealthy mulatto. While both Mary Ellen and her husband were mulattos, they each could pass as white.

The couple soon became allied with the Underground Railroad, helping slaves escape to freedom by various routes, but mainly on the railroad from Nova Scotia to Virginia (near Harper's Ferry).

James died suddenly. There were some who felt his death came at Mary Ellen's hand. Nevertheless, he left Mary Ellen a wealthy woman.

Pleasant continued her rescue work for the slaves by sneaking onto plantations and soon became a much-hunted rescue worker. She fled to New Orleans to hide out with the family of her second husband.

In New Orleans, Mary Ellen had the opportunity to study with social-activist Voodoo Queen Mam'zelle, Marie Laveau. Laveau had invented a way to use Voodoo to aid the disenfranchised, and Mary Ellen wanted to learn it.

The strategy she learned was how to use the secrets of the rich to get aid for the poor, a "model" that would serve her well in San Francisco.

Slave owners continued on her trail, and Mary Ellen was forced to head west. She arrived in San Francisco April 7, 1852. The population at the time was about 40,000 people. To serve them there were 700 gambling establishments.

It was not a safe place, with five murders occurring every six days.

The California Fugitive Slave Act stipulated that anyone without freedom papers could be captured and returned to slavery. Mary Ellen took two identities to conceal the fact that she had no papers.

As Mrs. Ellen Smith, she worked as a white boardinghouse steward-cook. As Mrs. Pleasant, she continued her work to help her people escape from slavery.

Working as Mrs. Smith, she was able to get jobs and privileges for "colored" people in San Francisco. She gained the nickname, "The Black City Hall." As Mrs. Pleasant, she used her money to help ex-slaves fight unfair laws and to get lawyers or business in California.

Mary Ellen became an expert capitalist. Her own assets grew, and she prospered. But when European emigrants began taking the menial jobs, anti-black sentiment and national depression mounted.

She traveled east again to help John Brown end slavery forever. Their plans involved dangerous ventures. Mary Ellen wrote, "I'd rather be a corpse than a coward."

John Brown was hanged for his efforts, and Mary Ellen narrowly escaped.

Back in California, she continued to fight. When the Emancipation Proclamation and the California Right-of-Testimony of 1863, were passed, Mary Ellen openly declared her race.

She orchestrated court battles to challenge the right of testimony, and in 1868, her battle for the right to ride the San Francisco trolleys set a precedent in the California Supreme Court.

Mary Ellen is said to have amassed a fortune of thirty million.

When Montgomery Street auctioneers put Lola Montez' jewels up for sale, Mammy Pleasant was the principal purchaser.

In San Francisco, the Barbary Coast was confined to Pacific Street. Never-the-less, the price of properties several blocks away declined because of their proximity to the Pacific Street brothels.

The ambitious Mammy Pleasant bought a number of these depressed properties, sure that as growth in the city occurred, so would the value of the property.

She was right. Anything on Montgomery and Kearney Streets between Washington and Broadway, appreciated.

Mary Ellen, without appearing on the scene personally, moved a madam and her girls out of one ramshackle house on Kearney Street, rebuilt it, and spent fifteen-thousand-dollars furnishing it as a luxurious parlor house.

As far as the public knew, the parlor house was owned by the madam who leased the house from Mammy Pleasant, a "Madam Em" or "French Em".

It is claimed that Mary Ellen stopped at nothing in her unrelenting drive for wealth and power. Harry Sinclair Drago, author of *Notorious Ladies of the Frontier,* said, "At least on four occasions, she took girls out of the houses of prostitution, transformed them into young ladies with a veneer of culture, and married them off to rich men."

31

The Black Widow

As long as there has been a Hollywood, there's been a Hollywood madam.

During the "golden" age of the 1920s and 1930s, Hollywood madams could count on the cops giving them enough warning to clear out any customers.

The renowned Lee Francis always had French Champagne chilled and dishes of Russian caviar waiting for the vice squad when they arrived. After the squad went through the motion of searching for prostitutes or their Johns, the officers would sit down to enjoy Lee Francis' hospitality.

Lee Francis was hit with a morality charge and spent 30 days in jail. A lady by the name of Ann Forrester took over the business. She was dubbed as "The Black Widow".

By the late 1930s, the "Black Widow's prostitution business was raking in $5,000 a week. Ann Forrester soon got her own citation.

While the Black Widow sat in jail, her protégé Brenda Allen opened shop. She reigned as the bawdy house empress of L.A. vice, serving millionaires and movie stars alike.

She boasted that she had never spent a day in jail. One reason for this is that she had taken a Hollywood vice cop, Sgt. Elmer V. Jackson, as her lover and business partner.

In 1948, Brenda Allen too, was indicted after an LAPD tap recorded a business chat between the bordello madam and her cop lover. Talk circulated immediately about a possible black book containing the names of 250 celebrity guests.

The vice sting embarrassed the Los Angeles Police Department even more. Allen's black book included not only her lover Jackson, but other vice cops paid to protect prostitutes.

Allen rented large, ornate party houses above Sunset Strip on streets such as Cory Avenue, Harold Way, and Miller Place. After one arrest, she simply moved to another house on the next street.

32

Assaults on Prostitutes In Virginia City, Nevada

Women were often assaulted in Virginia City. Being a prostitute, dance hall girl, or a beer server in the wild mining town was truly a hazard for women.

Danger was especially prevalent in the Red-Light district of D street. While some women were capable of defending themselves, others were not.

In November 1863, a rowdy group of men went into Kunstler's Hall on C Street for drinks. The young woman brought their drinks and one of the men struck her, knocking her down and leaving here with a black eye.

The drunken man's actions caused a frenzy with the crowd. Some men pulled their knives while other produced a pistol in defense of the fallen woman. The bartender sent for the police. The crowd scurried out.

By the time they had arrived however, there was no one left to arrest.

In 1864 a group of ladies who had been shopping walked along C street. When they neared the International Hotel, however, a group of fellows started hurling snowballs at them.

Two of the women drew their revolvers and began shooting at the men.

Nobody was hurt, but two officers came to the scene and arrested the two women. When they came before the judge, he dismissed them both.

Another incident in February of 1867, Police Officer Billings came upon a group of boys under the influence of liquor. They were playing practical jokes on each other.

When officer Billings came near, the boys attacked him. One lad threw an egg and hit him in the ear. Several others grabbed him and blackened his face with burnt cork.

Another grabbed Officer Billing's pistol and waved it around. Chief Edwards arrived on the scene and arrested several of the boys. Their bail was set at $1,000.

When officers knocked on the door of Florence Donreath's house of prostitution, a man answered the door. He threatened to kill the officers if they tried to enter. He closed the door in their faces.

The officers broke down the door and arrested everyone in sight. Florence had been an alcoholic trouble maker and had been arrested many times.

Florence died of delirium tremens near the Crystal Peak Dance Hall and Saloon.

33

The Arizona Girls

The men in Tombstone didn't hesitate to brag about their women. They claimed they were superior in charity, decorum, honesty and manners to those in Bisbee, Charleston and Tucson.

Most notable of Tombstone's madams was Cora Adams. The thing that set her house apart was her strict rule on honesty when it came to money. When a gentleman became noticeably drunk, Cora took his valuables and made two invoices, one for him and one for her.

When he called it a night, she returned his valuables.

Tombstone also had Blonde Mary, Big Minnie, and Madame Mustache.

Prostitution was an integral part of the building and funding of Tombstone. In 1881, Mayor John Clum allowed prostitution to exist in the residential areas and not just in the red-light district.

The town drew interesting characters, such as "Big Nose Kate", often a consort of Doc Holiday. Kate, whose name was Mary Katherine Horony, established the first brothel in Tombstone.

The madams had to be tough and business savvy in Tombstone and they had to be caring to their girls.

Darba Jo Butler, a tour-guide at the Bird Cage theatre, says there was a very dark side to the industry. "They came here to sew dresses, to look for a husband, to open a business. Unfortunately, if they didn't have somebody to support them, they were trapped."

Butler noted there were a lot of suicides and a lot of drug use. There was just a lot of unhappiness associated with it.

"A lot of the girls that worked in the Bird Cage were also the first to step up to help charities," Butler said."

Nancy Sosa, a historian in Tombstone, said she thought the prostitution angle was over-played to please the tourists.

"If prostitution was truly as rampant as people say it was, we would find a lot more arrests in the docket. The myth is a lot more entertaining than the truth."

34

The Rolodex Madam

When Karen L. Wilkening walked out of California's Rehabilitation Center in Norco, California, her public relations man was already there in a plush silver limousine for her grand departure.

Wilkening was convicted in San Diego for running a prostitution establishment.

She was dubbed the Rolodex Madam for her list of 500 clients. She was set to hold a much-touted press conference.

Lt. George Giurbino, administrative assistant, at the medium-security prison said, "Usually we don't set up this type of situation. A lot of times the inmates don't want to be interviewed."

When the 45-year old madam emerged, she was both tearful and glowing in a black and gold dress.

There were more than a dozen cameramen and reporters corralled behind a yellow police line.

Wilkening was different. She said she had plenty to say. Before she said a thing, however, she said she wanted a green salad and a glimpse of the sea.

She noted she hadn't seen the ocean in two years, and she was most anxious to "have some serenity."

Vice officers raided her high-class call-girl ring and confiscated her Rolodex file in 1987. She then fled the country to avoid prosecution on 28 counts of pimping and pandering.

Ray Drasnin, her publicist, said her Rolodex list included the names of well-known San Diegans, including bankers, doctors and lawyers. At the time of her release, Wilkening had only named one such personality, the late actor Desi Arnaz.

Prominent San Diego car dealer Tony McCune testified in court at her preliminary hearing that he was one of her customers.

San Diego's police department spent $20,000 tracking Wilkening. She was found in Manila, in the Philippines. The police not only wanted to question the madam on the 28 charges against her, but also on the deaths of 44 prostitutes and transients.

Wilkening briefly shared a cell with Elizabeth (Betty) Roddick, a La Jolla socialite that admitted killing her husband and his new wife.

She obtained early release from Norco's medium security prison with good time credits. She said, "What lies ahead, I'm not sure yet. I'm starting over from scratch.

"I would like to think there are some people out there with some guts and a sense of humor who might consider hiring me."

Wilkening, who was once paid $150 an hour for providing prostitutes, was paid 24 cents an hour in prison to work as a literary tutor. She also has training as an algebra teacher, a systems analyst and a management consultant.

She published her own story in 1991. She noted that she married a Navy pilot stationed at North Island, just outside San Diego. I married a boy from my high school back home in Long Island, New York.

He came home as a plebe from Annapolis at Christmas in his dress uniform and swept me off my feet. We were married for four and a half years. After her divorce, Karen stayed in San Diego.

In early 1961, a former associate suggested she meet a friend who was selling a business. Karen took her resume to meet the person who was selling an escort service.

Basically, what she sold me was her client base and her girls, some of whom were dancers for bachelor parties. The business had no name and was not advertised.

While she turned over a number of girls for me, I soon had all new ones. There were former school teachers, nurses, secretaries, a lot of students and jazzy housewives.

One client was a paraplegic in his 20s. He had a terrible accident and had been married, but his wife left him.

His father had compassion and made arrangement to have his son continue with his sex life.

Another young client had cerebral palsy. His mother called about once a month and made arrangements for him.

Karen was raided by nine policemen. They ordered her to sit on her couch. When she asked if she could get a coat from her closet, they got very upset. "Maybe they thought I had a gun in there."

My Rolodex file was in the kitchen cabinet because I didn't need to use it all the time. It was my address list of everyone I've known my who life.

It had my old boyfriends, my banker, real estate associates, the person who fixed my car, my hairdresser and a lot of other addresses, mostly inactive.

I heard someone in the kitchen yell "bingo". They found my Rolodex in which I had a San Diego patrolman listed. He had called several times for dancers for bachelor parties.

The cops took every penny that Karen had, which was approximately $900. They took her answering machine, and the tape that was in it. She watched the Rolodex going out the door.

When there were no more cops in my house, she locked the door, knowing she had to get out of there. The only option she had to stop the prosecution was for her to disappear.

The Philippines seemed like the best place to find a new identity.

That was until immigration officials came calling in the Philippines and arrested Karen for passport violations. Immigration officials gave her the option of fighting deportation. She decided to face the consequences and returned home.

Meet the Author

Alton Pryor

Alton Pryor has published fifty-plus books since turning 70 in 1997—many of them about California's past and the colorful characters who rode our trails to fame or infamy.

To date he has sold more than 500,000-plus copies of his first book, "Little Known Tales in California History" and has done respectably well with most of his other titles.

Until fate derailed his 33-year journalism career, he never aspired to write a book, and certainly never anticipated he would come to be regarded as "Mr. Self-Publishing" by his peers in the Sacramento area. "I would have liked living in the Old West," he says. "I wanted, at one time, to be a really good cowboy. I had horses as a young man and even took a raw colt and trained it to work cattle."

He early learned that farming wasn't for him, but that writing was his real passion. He was terminated after writing for 27 years for a magazine. The magazine was sold to a Midwest firm.

Alton turned to writing books and says now, "I wish I had been fired 20 years earlier."

Index

166

Mary Ellen Pleasant, 6, 143
Mary Jane slippers, 16
Mattie Silks, 6, 123, 126
Mayor Jim Rolph, 51
Mayor Jimmy Rolph, 25
Medford, Oregon, 19, 20
Merced County, 78, 79, 80
Mona Regan, 84
Mona's lesbian joint, 23
Monterrey. Mexico, 112
Mother Damnable, 107
Mt. Pisgah Cemetery, 113
Munich, 120
Nancy Sosa, 156
Nederland, Colorado, 117
New Orleans, 97, 98, 131, 134, 144
New York City, 121, 139
Nob Hill, 23, 30, 51
O'Farrell Street, 14, 25
Oklahoma, 124

Old West, 109, 163
Oregon State Prison, 21
Oregon Trail, 19
Painless Parker, 74
Painted Ladies, 6, 109
Patrick Purdy Hall, 121
Paul Bouquet Cohen, 74
Paul Verdier, 24
Pearl de Vere, 110, 111
Pickwick Stage, 20
Pimps, 12
Pineapple McFarland, 43
Pleasure Den, 36
Plymouth Rock, 17
Portland, 20
Portuguese, 107
Poverty Gulch, 112
Presidio, 83
Prohibition, 13
Prostitution, 12, 125, 156
Quick-Heating Electric Iron, 21
Red Clark, 73, 74
Regal Amber Brewery, 73
Reggie Gamble, 27

Made in the USA
Coppell, TX
09 January 2022

71327545R00096